TEEN

®

T

CONTENT RATED BY
ESRB

World of Warcraft requires access to the Internet and acceptance of the World of Warcraft Terms of Use Agreement. Requires subscription to play. Internet connection required. Additional Online fees may apply, and player is responsible for all applicable internet fees.

WARNING - SEIZURES

A small percentage of people may experience a seizure or blackout triggered by light patterns, flashing lights, or other images that appear in computer games. If you have an epileptic condition, consult your physician before installing or playing this game. Even people who have no history of epilepsy may experience a seizure while viewing a computer game.

A seizure can be accompanied by any of the following symptoms: altered vision, convulsions, disorientation, eye or muscle twitching, involuntary movements, or loss of movement.

If you experience any of these symptoms, immediately stop playing and consult a doctor.

Parents or guardians of children playing this game should monitor their children closely. If your child suffers any of these symptoms, stop playing the game immediately and consult a doctor.

2.86

Blizzard Entertainment
P.O. Box 18979, Irvine, CA 92623

(800) 953-SNOW	Direct Sales
(949) 955-0283	International Direct Sales
(949) 955-1382	Technical Support
(800) 59-BLIZZARD	Billing and Account Services
http://www.blizzard.com	World Wide Web
wowtech@blizzard.com	Technical Support
billing@blizzard.com	Billing and Account Services

CONTENTS

Chapter 1
Installing the Game (PC)

System Requirements

OS: Windows 98/ME/2000/XP

Processor: Intel Pentium3 800MHz, or AMD Duron 800MHz

Memory: 256MB RAM

Video:

> **Minimum:** 32MB 3D graphics processor with Hardware Transform and Lighting, such as an NVIDIA GeForce 2 class card or above.
>
> **Recommended:** 64MB 3D graphics processor with Vertex and Pixel Shader capability, such as an NVIDIA GeForce FX 5700 class card or above.
>
> For a complete list of supported 3D cards, please visit: **http://www.blizzard.com/support/wow**

Sound: DirectX compatible sound card

Install Size: 4 gigabytes of free Hard Disk space

Installation Instructions

Place the World of Warcraft CD into your CD-ROM or DVD-ROM drive. If your computer is autoplay enabled, an installation window will automatically pop up on your Windows desktop. Click the Install World of Warcraft button and follow the on-screen instructions to install World of Warcraft to your hard drive.

If the installation window does not appear, open the My Computer icon on your desktop and double-click on the drive letter corresponding to your CD-ROM or DVD-ROM drive to open it. Double-click on the Install.exe icon in the CD-ROM contents and follow the on-screen instructions to install World of Warcraft.

Inserting Multiple CDs

World of Warcraft comes on 4 CDs. During installation, you will be prompted to insert additional CDs to continue installation. Open your CD-ROM or DVD-ROM drive, insert the requested CD, and click on the OK button to resume installation.

Installing DirectX

You will need to install DirectX 9.0c in order to properly run World of Warcraft. During installation you will be prompted to install DirectX if you do not already have the most up-to-date version installed on your computer.

Installing the Game (Mac)

System Requirements

OS: Mac OS X 10.3.5 or newer required

Processor: 933MHz G4/G5 processor

RAM: 512MB RAM, DDR RAM recommended

Video: ATI or NVIDIA graphics processor with 32MB VRAM, 64MB recommended

Controls: A keyboard and mouse are required. Input devices other than a mouse and keyboard are not supported

Install Size: 4 gigabytes of free Hard Disk space

Installation Instructions

Place the World of Warcraft CD into your CD-ROM or DVD-ROM drive. Double-click on the World of Warcraft CD icon. Then double-click on the installer application to copy the required game files to your hard drive.

Inserting Multiple CDs

World of Warcraft comes on 4 CDs. During installation, you will be prompted to insert additional CDs to continue installation. Open your CD-ROM or DVD-ROM drive, insert the requested CD, and follow the onscreen instructions to resume installation.

Single Button Mice

With a single-button mouse, hold down the Command key on the keyboard while you click the mouse button to simulate a right-click in the game.

ALL PLATFORMS

Setting up an Account

You must create an account before you can play World of Warcraft. Chapter 2: Account Setup and Billing, has instructions on how to create an account, as well as information on billing and account support.

Connectivity

You must have an active Internet connection to play World of Warcraft.

Modem: 56K or better

Mouse

Multi button mouse with scroll wheel recommended.

TROUBLESHOOTING

If you experience any trouble running World of Warcraft, be sure to read the most recent readme.txt and patch notes text files. These files detail the latest changes and any bug fixes made to the game. Your problem might already be listed there, along with possible solutions.

Many times, errors in running the game can be attributed to a lack of updated drivers. Ensure that the drivers for all your hardware are up to date before contacting Blizzard Entertainment for customer support.

GENERAL TROUBLESHOOTING [PC]

General Lockups/Video Problems

If your computer hard locks without an error message, reboots during game play, will not start, or has distorted graphics of any sort, please make sure you have the latest video card drivers for your 3D accelerator. Contact your hardware manufacturer to find the latest drivers available, or check our Driver Update Information page on our support website for links to the most common hardware vendors at **http://www.blizzard.com/support/wow**

Sound Issues

If you are experiencing sound distortions, periodic loss of sound, loud squelches, whistles, or pops, confirm that you have the latest version of DirectX installed on your system. Also, verify that your sound drivers are compatible with the newest version of DirectX. Contact your hardware manufacturer to find the latest drivers available, or check our Driver Update Information page on our support website for links to the most common hardware vendors at **http://www.blizzard.com/support/wow**

General Troubleshooting [Mac]

Most lockups, video problems, or sound problems can be solved by installing the latest available software updates from Apple. All of the latest video and sound drivers are included in the OS available from Software Update from the Apple menu.

You can find additional troubleshooting instructions at: **http://www.blizzard.com/support/wow/**

TECHNICAL SUPPORT CONTACTS

Web Support

The Blizzard Entertainment Technical Support website has solutions to the most common game questions and problems. This free service is available 24 hours a day, 7 days a week. You can find our Technical Support website located at: **http://www.worldofwarcraft.com/support**

Email Support

You can email the Technical Support department at any time at **wowtech@blizzard.com**. Under normal circumstances you will receive an automated reply within 15 minutes, detailing solutions to the most common problems. You will receive a second email sent typically between 24 to 72 hours later, containing a more detailed solution to your particular problem or question.

Automated Phone Support

Our automated phone support is offered 24 hours a day, 7 days a week and has an 80% success rate at addressing the most common questions and concerns. To use this automated phone support, please call **(949) 955-1382.** Automated support carries no charge beyond any normal long distance charges from your phone company for calls outside of your local area.

Live Phone Support

We offer live phone support Monday through Friday 9 A.M. to 6 P.M., Pacific Standard Time (except on U.S. holidays). Contact our Technical Support staff by calling us at **(949) 955-1382**. This form of support carries no charge other than any normal long distance charges from your phone company for calls outside of your local area. **NO GAME-PLAYING HINTS WILL BE GIVEN THROUGH THIS NUMBER.** Please be sure to consult our troubleshooting section before calling Technical Support, and be near your computer if possible when calling.

Note

For updated information about protecting your computer and World of Warcraft account, along with answers to commonly asked questions and additional troubleshooting material, go to **http://www.worldofwarcraft.com/support**

Game Hints

If you are seeking a game tip, hint, or additional game information for World of Warcraft, please visit: **http://www.worldofwarcraft.com**

Game Performance

If you encounter slow or choppy game play, there are several game options that can be adjusted to improve performance. These options are accessible via the Video Options Menu. Selecting a lower resolution, decreasing the FarClip, World Detail, and Animation settings will have the greatest effect.

Chapter 2
Account Setup and Billing

CREATING AN ACCOUNT

After you have successfully installed World of Warcraft, start a game by double-clicking on the World of Warcraft icon on your desktop. You can also start a game from the Start menu.

Once you start the game, you are taken to the Login screen. After agreeing to the Terms of Use (see below), you will see a blank Login field and a blank Password field in the middle of the screen. Below that is a "Create Account" button. Click on this button to setup an account.

You will immediately be taken out of the game and back to your desktop. Your web browser will automatically open and take you to the World of Warcraft account creation web page. Follow the instructions on the web page to successfully create an account.

When you are finished, return to the World of Warcraft Main Login screen, enter your Login and Password in the appropriate fields, and press the Enter World button. You are now ready to play World of Warcraft.

Terms of Use Agreement

The first time you load World of Warcraft, a Terms of Use Agreement will appear on your screen before you can progress to the Login screen. To play the game, you must read the agreement in its entirety and click the Agree button. The Agree button is grayed out initially, but becomes enabled when you scroll to the end of the agreement. After agreeing to the Terms of Use, you are allowed to play the game. If you refuse the Terms of Use, you cannot play the game. Anytime the Terms of Use Agreement is updated, it will reappear when you next start the game. You must read it again and click the Agree button to progress to the Login screen.

Internet Connection

World of Warcraft is a massively-multiplayer online role-playing game. That means it is played entirely online and has no offline component. You must have an active Internet connection to play this game.

Blizzard is not responsible for any fees you may incur from your internet service provider that are in addition to your monthly World of Warcraft subscription fee.

BILLING

When you purchase World of Warcraft, you also get a free trial period during which you can play the game free of charge. At the end of this trial, you will have to assume the monthly subscription fee in order to continue playing World of Warcraft.

Payment Methods

During your account creation, you must specify your method of payment. You can pay your monthly fees by credit card, with pre-paid time cards sold by Blizzard Entertainment online and in local game stores, or by other methods depending on your location.

Account and Billing Issues

If you have any questions or issues dealing with billing or your World of Warcraft account, please contact Billing and Account Services. Our representatives can help you with many issues, including:

- ♦ Questions regarding billing
- ♦ Registering or setting up an account
- ♦ Recovering your account or password
- ♦ Canceling your account
- ♦ Reactivating a canceled account
- ♦ Or any other Account or Billing issues

We offer live phone support Monday through Friday 9 A.M. to 6 P.M. PST (Hours may be extended due to peak workloads). This form of support carries no charge other than any normal long distance charges from your phone company for calls outside of your local area. NO GAME PLAY HITS WILL BE GIVEN THROUGH THIS NUMBER.

You can contact us by email at **billing@blizzard.com** or by phone at **1-800-59-BLIZZARD (1-800-592-5499)**.

Chapter 3

Getting Started

If this is your first time playing a massively multiplayer online role-playing game, then you may find this chapter helpful. It will walk you through creating a character and playing through your first level in the game.

Many of the game concepts introduced in this tutorial are explained in greater detail in later chapters of the manual. If you are unclear about game terms, be sure to read the glossary of terms and acronyms in Chapter 11: Community.

Note

World of Warcraft, like many massively-multiplayer online role-playing games, is constantly evolving. In an effort to keep the game challenging and balanced, Blizzard will occasionally implement changes to the game through patches. In some cases, new content and game systems will also be added. At the time of the printing of this manual, the information contained herein was accurate and relevant. However, as the designers do adjust the game from time to time to give you the best gaming experience possible, some information in this manual might no longer be current.

To see last-minute amendments to the game, read the readme.txt file on the CD. This file records all changes made to World of Warcraft just prior to release that were too late to include in the manual.

Also be sure to check out the latest patch notes and updated information on the World of Warcraft strategy page at **http://www.worldofwarcraft.com**. The website is continuously updated to reflect the most current version of the game and includes more detailed information on the topics covered in this manual.

Creating Your Character

You've created an account to play World of Warcraft (WoW) and have entered the game for the first time. At the character creation screen, you have many options for making your first character.

Choose Your Race

Your first choice when making a character is your race. The eight races in WoW are divided into two factions: the Horde and the Alliance. At one time in Azeroth's past, the Horde was a force of evil, and the Alliance was a bastion of good. However, in today's war-torn Azeroth, such black and white distinctions are gone. Both factions are simply fighting to preserve their way of life in the wake of the Chaos War.

Each faction has four races. The Alliance is comprised of the dwarves, gnomes, humans, and night elves, while the Horde consists of the orcs, tauren, trolls, and undead. Each race has a unique set of characteristics and its own list of available class choices. Some of the different races also begin in their own unique starting area, while others share a beginning region.

Note

When choosing a race, remember that you can only interact meaningfully with members of your own faction. When dealing with races of the opposite faction, your interaction options are much more limited, and sometimes, hostile. If you wish to play with your friends, you should choose races on the same side.

Read the descriptions to the left to learn more about each race before you arrive at your decision.

Choose Your Class

After choosing your race, it's time to select a class. There are nine classes in the game, and each has its own unique set of abilities and powers. These nine are the druid, hunter, mage, paladin, priest, rogue, shaman, warrior and warlock. Not every class is available to every race.

Although each class is unique, they do fall into general categories. Warriors and rogues engage in melee combat, and have special abilities but no spells. The priest is a potent healer, while the mage is a powerful offensive caster. The hunter and warlock both excel in dealing damage, and also have pets to support them. Druids are a class with a variety of spells, including healing, but they also have shapeshifting powers as well. The paladin is a class with melee capability, healing, and defensive spells that is available only to Alliance races. The shaman is a hybrid class capable of healing, supporting group members, and fighting in melee. It is available only to Horde races.

If you want more detailed information on each class before you decide, refer to Chapter 6: Races and Classes.

Choose Your Gender

You can be a male or female character in World of Warcraft. Men and women are equal in Azeroth, so the only differences between the two genders are cosmetic.

Choose Your Appearance

When making a character, you can customize his appearance by adjusting his skin color, the look of his face, hair style, hair color, and facial hair. You can create hundreds of unique appearances with the different combinations, or If you want the game to create a random appearance, click on the "Randomize" button. To get a better view of your character, you can click the left and right arrows at the bottom of the screen. These arrows let you rotate your character 360 degrees.

Name Your Character

Now name your character by typing his name in the field at the bottom of the screen. Your name can only contain letters and must be 2 to 12 characters in length. Have several choices ready because your first choice might already be taken. Choose your names wisely as accounts with bad names may be changed or terminated. For more information about our naming policy, go to **http://www.worldofwarcraft.com/policy/naming.shtml**

Enter the World

After creating and naming your character, click the Create button, and if the name is not already taken, your character is ready. The next time you enter the character screen, your character will be waiting for you. Click on it now, and press the "Enter World" button.

After watching a movie introducing your racial heritage, you appear in a small village in the wilderness.

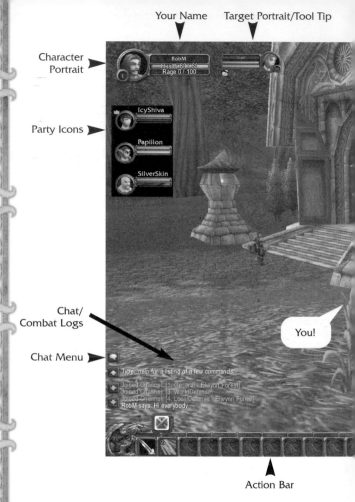

Your Name   Target Portrait/Tool Tip

Character Portrait

Party Icons

Chat/ Combat Logs

Chat Menu

You!

Action Bar

Understanding Your Interface

The main screen is the first thing you see when you enter the actual world of Warcraft. In the middle of the screen is your character, while the rest of the view is occupied by your environment.

You can adjust this view by using your mouse wheel, or by pressing the Home and End buttons. To zoom in your view and see through a first-person perspective, push your mouse wheel forward.

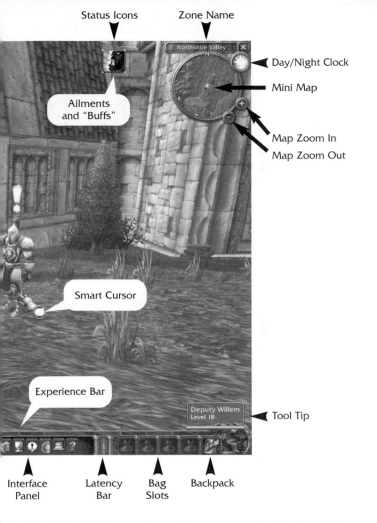

Status Icons

Zone Name

Northshire Valley

Day/Night Clock

Mini Map

Map Zoom In

Map Zoom Out

Ailments and "Buffs"

Smart Cursor

Experience Bar

Deputy Willem
Level 18

Tool Tip

Interface Panel

Latency Bar

Bag Slots

Backpack

To pull back for a bird's-eye view, roll your mouse wheel backward. You can also slowly roll your mouse wheel to arrive at a view setting in between these two extremes.

You can rotate the camera around your character by clicking on an empty part of the screen and moving the mouse while holding down the left button. You can tilt the camera up or down by doing the same.

Description of User Interface Items

Action Bar: Holds any spells or abilities you place here from your Spellbook and Abilities window. Once placed, they can be activated with a quick hotkey or mouse click.

Ailments: Any negative conditions, or debuffs, on your character appear here. Such ailments usually are inflicted upon you by monsters you are fighting.

Bag Slots: Your inventory in the game. All items not equipped on your character are stored here. One backpack is automatically provided for you. To fill the other four slots, you must purchase, find, or make additional bags.

Character Portrait: Shows your character name, face, level, and health bar. Depending on your class, the second bar could be your mana, rage, or energy bar.

Chat Button: Click on this button to access party and guild chats, private messaging of individual players, emotes, and voiced speech. Many of these same chat options are also available through hotkeys or commands that you can type at the chat prompt.

Chat Log: All chat messages appear here, along with miscellaneous character messages. You can scroll up or down this log by clicking the arrows, and jump to the latest message by clicking on the bottom button.

Chat Prompt: Type here to send messages to other players or to the general area. Press the "Enter" key to open it.

Combat Log: All messages related to combat appear in this window. Watch it during combat to see how you are affecting your opponent, and vice versa.

Day/Night Clock: This clock shows you the time of day if you mouse over it.

Experience Bar: Shows your current experience point total and how much you need to reach next level.

Interface Panel: These tabs enable you to access your character information, spellbook and abilities window, character talents, quest log, world map, social options, the main menu, and GM support.

Latency Bar: Measures the speed of your connection to the World of Warcraft server. A green bar means your connection is good. A yellow bar means you may experience intermittent delay, called lag. A red bar means your connection is poor and you will experience significant delay.

Name: The name of your selected target. A tag underneath a name might be a player's guild affiliation.

Rest Marker: Shows your rest state. In rested state, you earn 200 percent of experience from kills. In normal state, you earn 100 percent of experience. Rest state does not affect quest or exploration experience.

Selection Circle: This circle appears around a target when you select it. The color of the circle indicates hostility. Red = Aggressive. Yellow = Passive until you attack. Green = Non-combatant.

Tool Tip: This appears when you click on or mouse over a creature or character. Inside is the target's name, level, and class or type. The color of the tool tip indicates hostility. Aggressive targets are red, passive targets that fights when struck first are yellow, non-hostile targets that cannot be attacked are green, and player characters are white.

Minimap: A miniature map of your character's surroundings. You can zoom the view in or out using the plus and minus keys. The name of your current zone or location appears above the minimap. Towns appear on the edge of the minimap as arrows, while party members, pets, and resource nodes appear as dots within the minimap.

Smart Cursor: When your mouse cursor moves over an object or character that you can interact with, it changes shape to reflect a new action you can perform. See page 44 for more info.

Status Icons: Any positive conditions, or buffs, affecting your character appear here. Most buffs are cast on you by yourself, friendly players, or NPCs.

Target Portrait: Shows the name, face, and health bar of any creature or character you click on in the game. Depending on the target, it might also have a mana, rage, or energy bar.

Moving In the World

After you acquaint yourself with the interface, it's time to move around the world.

You move your character primarily using the keyboard. Movement for forward, backward, turning left, and turning right, are already mapped onto the w, s, a, and d keys, as well as the arrow keys. Turning left and right means your character turns, thus changing the camera view, but your character does not actually move left or right. To move left or right, you can use the q and e keys, or you can hold down the right mouse button and press a or d. You will then run to one side or the other while facing forward. This sort of running is referred to as strafing.

To toggle auto-run, press the Num Lock key.

You can jump while moving by pressing the spacebar. To sit, press the x key. All your movement commands, as well as other commands, can be customized from the Key Bindings menu in the main menu.

Interacting with NPCs

Standing in front of you will be one or more non-player characters (NPCs). Mouse over one and you will see his name and occupation appear in a pop up box called the tool tip in the bottom right corner of your screen. Mouse over any other nearby NPCs to see who and what they are as well.

One or more of the NPCs in front of you will have a yellow exclamation point over their heads. This mark indicates that they are quest givers. If you mouse over other NPCs, you will find that some are trainers, vendors, or guards. If you can interact with an NPC, your cursor will change to a chat balloon or an icon representing the action you can perform with the NPC. A trainer, for instance, who offers extra learning for your class, is represented by a book cursor. A vendor, who sells you items, is represented by a bag.

To talk to or interact with any NPC, simply right-click on it. A box or window will then appear on your screen with instructions or options for you to act on.

Acquiring Quests from NPCs

Talk to the first quest giver NPC in your view. You'll notice that your cursor now appears as a chat balloon. When you right-click on the quest giver, it will begin talking to you through a dialog box. This dialog box is where you will read about the NPC's quest, what objectives you need to accomplish to complete the quest, and what reward, if any, you'll garner for your success. Many of the quests in your beginning area are simple. The quest givers here will ask you to slay some simple beasts to prove your mettle, gather items off of the environment or fallen creatures, or deliver letters to other NPCs.

To accept a quest, click on the Accept Quest button at the bottom of the quest dialog box.

You'll notice now that the yellow exclamation over the quest giver has changed to a gray question mark. The question mark tells you that this NPC is who you need to return to when you finish the objectives for your quest. However, the gray color indicates that you are not yet ready to speak to the quest giver because you haven't completed your goals.

Tracking Your Quests

No matter what race or class you play, you should have several quests to accomplish after talking to the various NPCs in your starting area. To help you keep track of your many quests, World of Warcraft offers the quest log. Mouse over the goblet at the bottom of the screen in the interface panel. The info box that pops up tells you this is the quest log. The letter "L" in parentheses is the hotkey that corresponds to the quest log. Click on the goblet or press "L" to open the log.

All the quests you have acquired will be listed here under a heading that corresponds to your starting zone. Clicking on a quest calls up a short synopsis of the quest, the quest description, and the quest reward. If you need to remind yourself of information regarding a quest, always look in your quest log first. Rereading the quest description will often give you the clues you seek.

Accomplishing Your First Quest

At least one of your first quests calls for you to slay some monsters to prove your mettle. The type of beasts will vary depending on your starting region: Gnomes and dwarves in Coldridge valley must slay rockjaw troggs, while orcs and trolls in the Valley of Trials must slay mottled boars. Other races will have other required targets.

Now head out into the wilderness around your starting region to hunt for these monsters.

Looking at Creatures

When you see the monster you must kill, mouse over it. Each time your mouse passes over a creature, its tool tip appears in the bottom right corner of your screen. As with NPC tool tips, this box shows you the monster's name, level, and type. The color of the tool tip is also very important to take notice of. If the color of the box is red, then the monster is hostile and will attack you on sight if you get close enough. If the color is yellow, then the creature is passive, meaning you can walk by it and not provoke attack. However, passive creatures will fight back if you attack them.

Your First Battle

Left-click on the monster to select it. Now you can rush up and right-click on it to attack!

Notice that after selecting the monster that its portrait shows up at the top of the screen next to your own, so you can monitor its health as you fight. A circle also appears around the monster, telling you that it is now selected. Notice that the color of the circle matches the color of the monster's tool tip.

The monster will now have closed to melee range. Whether you are a warrior or spellcaster, now you are engaged in close-range combat. As you are fighting, the attack icon in the first slot of your action bar is flashing. That means you are attacking a foe.

Spellcasting Delays and Interruptions

If you are a spellcaster, you can try to cast a spell in melee combat, but if you get hit, your spell might get interrupted or delayed. In addition, once you cast a spell, there is a brief delay before you can cast it again. Watch your action bar closely. Any ability you use will become grayed out once you use it. You have to wait for the ability or spell to brighten before you use it again. Depending on the spell or ability, this wait can be very short or very long.

Using Hotkeys to Fight

Although you began this fight by using your mouse to right-click on the monster, you can also fight using hotkeys. A hotkey is a key stroke that is mapped to an action, allowing you to perform that action by pressing the appropriate key instead of navigating through the user interface to find the action and then click on it with the mouse. For instance, if you are close to a monster and want to attack it, you can either right-click on it, or press the 1 key on your keyboard, which corresponds to the attack icon on the first slot in your action bar. If you had a spell or ability in the second slot, pressing the 2 key would activate that spell or ability.

Experience

When the monster dies, it collapses to the ground, and a number appears over your head. This is the experience point award you just earned for killing the monster. This experience also appears in your chat log and your combat log.

The Experience Bar

Some purple has also appeared in the experience bar that runs across the bottom of your screen above the action bar. Mouse over it to see the reading, which tells you how much experience you have and how much experience you need to reach the next level. Each time you make a kill, explore a new locale, or complete a quest, you earn experience, which adds to this bar. When the bar is full, you gain a new level, and your experience bar resets to zero, while the amount you need for the next level grows.

Looting Your Kill

Turn back to the monster's corpse. Sparkles of light drift up from its body. That means you can loot it. Mouse over the corpse, and your cursor changes to a bag. Right-click on the corpse to open up the loot window.

Inside the loot window should be some items. If you killed a humanoid monster, such as a kobold, you would find money inside the window. If you killed a beast, like a wolf, you might find wolf parts. Keep in mind that you won't always get loot from a kill; some monsters carry nothing.

Right-click or left-click on the items in the loot window to pick them up. When you pick up the last item in the loot window, the loot window closes, and the sparkles disappear.

As soon as you loot the corpse, open your backpack. Inside one of the slots you will find the item you just looted. Multiple items will take up multiple slots, unless they are of the same type, in which case they might stack.

Recovering Health

While you were fighting, you lost some health. Now that you've looted your kill, you can rest. During a battle, be sure to monitor your health by watching your combat log and your health bar next to your portrait. In some cases, you might have to run away before you lose all your health and die.

All characters automatically recover health after combat at a gradual rate. This healing rate increases if you sit down. If you also eat while sitting, this healing rate improves even more dramatically.

Left-click or right-click on the food icon in the last slot of your action bar. Your character then sits and begins eating. While your character is eating, it gains back health rapidly. When it is finished eating, your character will be at full health and ready to attack more monsters.

Turning In Your First Quest

The quest you are trying to fulfill asks you to kill a certain number of monsters. When you have fulfilled the requirement and killed the necessary number, return to the NPC that gave you this quest. Whereas before you saw a gray question mark over that NPCs head, now you should see a yellow mark. The change in color tells you that you have accomplished your objectives and can turn in the quest.

Right-click on the NPC to open a dialog box and speak to it. Click on the Complete Quest button at the bottom of the box and your quest is erased from your quest log and a message in your chat log tells you that you finished the quest.

Upon turning in the quest, you'll gain a large experience point reward, which appears over your character, in your chat log, and in your combat log. Look at your experience bar and you will see that it has been filled with more experience.

If there was a material reward offered for the quest, it will be added to your backpack. If you had a choice of rewards, you will need to select one by clicking on it in the dialog box before you can click the Complete Quest button.

Collecting Items for a Quest

Now it's time to continue questing. Open your quest log. One quest asks you to collect a number of items for the NPC. These types of quests are called collection quests. In many cases, a collection quest can only be fulfilled by killing monsters and looting the necessary items from their corpses. Some collection quests, however, simply ask you to retrieve items from objects in the world. The first orc and troll collection quest, for example, asks you to bring back cactus apples from the numerous cactus plants dotting the Valley of Trials.

Go to the object that offers the desired collection item. In the case of an orc or troll player, this would be a cactus plant. In the case of any other player race, this would be the corpse of a monster you just killed. Your quest log description will always tell you exactly what monster you must kill in order to find the item. Always refer back to your quest log if you forget what monster drops the item you need.

To get the item, open up the object's loot window. Keep in mind that if you are looting a monster, you aren't always guaranteed an item. Don't worry. Quest collection items do drop fairly regularly. Keep killing monsters and you'll eventually collect the required number.

Pick up the item from the loot window and once you do so, a message on your screen tells you the item you just looted, how many of those items you now have, and how many you still need.

When you have collected the necessary number, turn in this quest for another experience award, and possibly a material reward as well.

Equipping Your Character

At least one of your beginning quests offers you a material reward that is a piece of armor. When you gain this reward, you want to equip it immediately.

Open your Character Info window by clicking on the small portrait of your character in the bottom of the screen or by pressing the hotkey "C."

Your character appears in the middle of the info window, with slots on either side of it. Mouse over these slots to see that they correspond to areas of the body where you can wear armor. Your Hands slot is empty.

Open your backpack, and left-click on the piece of armor in your backpack. The slot that you can place it in should now be glowing. Bring the cursor to that empty slot in your Character Info window, and click on the slot. The armor will then drop into the slot, improving your character's armor rating. Look at your character closely. Your character is now wearing the new armor.

Leveling Up

The experience you earned from killing monsters and completing your quests should fill up your experience bar. If not, kill a few more monsters or try to finish another quest. When your experience bar fills up, a congratulatory sound and a flourish of light tell you that you've just leveled up. Your chat log also congratulates you on gaining a level. Every time you level up, your character increases in power. Not only do you gain extra health, but you also gain increases to one or more of your primary attributes, such as agility or stamina. Spellcasters also gain mana when they level up.

Training Your Character

Now that you have gained a level, it's time to visit your class trainer

Characters gain access to new spells and abilities whenever they gain levels. To learn these new abilities, you must speak to your class trainer. Right-click on the trainer to open the Training window

Inside the window are all the abilities you could possibly learn. Abilities you can learn right away are green. Abilities that are beyond your current level are red. You can mouse over an ability to see what it does. If you can't learn it yet, mousing over it will tell you the minimum level requirement for that ability.

If you see any spell or ability that you can learn right now, click on it and then click the Learn button at the bottom of the Training window. Learning a new spell or ability always costs money.

If You Need Money

If you don't have enough money to buy a new spell or ability, sell some of your loot at a merchant. Merchants are identified as such in their tool tips. To buy or sell from them, right-click on them to open up their merchant window. Your backpack also opens at the same time. Right-click on an item you want to buy or sell and the money automatically trades hands. When you have the money you need, return to the trainer.

Adjusting Your Action Bar

After you learn a new ability or spell, it's time to add it to your action bar. This allows you to use it easily in battle. Click on the Abilities button on the bottom of your screen. This button looks like a book. You can also press the "I" hotkey.

In your Abilities window, you see your attack ability, along with any other abilities you already have. An ability that has the "passive" tag next to it does not need to be activated and is always on. These types of abilities never need to be placed on your action bar.

The ability you just learned should be on this ability page. If you learned a spell, it will be on the spell page. In some cases, you might have to click on the spell or ability tab at the bottom of your book to access it. Mouse over the new spell or ability icon in your spellbook or abilities book to see what it does. Then add it to your action bar. Left-click and hold the icon. Then drag it onto the third slot In your action bar. It now appears there. You can now use it by clicking on it or by pressing the appropriate hotkey, which is the 3 key.

Onto Greater Adventures

Now that you have secured greater equipment and grown in power, it is time to continue your adventures in Azeroth. Complete whatever quests remain for you in your starting area. Speak to all the non-player characters you can one last time, and at least one of them will offer you a quest to venture beyond your home to greater settlements beyond.

Take heart in the lessons you have learned and journey forth with courage. Good luck. The World of Warcraft awaits.

A Special Note on Dying

No matter how good an adventurer you are, eventually you will know the sting of death. Thankfully, death in the World of Warcraft isn't permanent.

Ghosts

When your health is reduced to 0 or less, through battle or accident, you die. A release window pops up over your corpse with a button you can press to release your spirit. If you choose the Release Spirit button or wait longer than five minutes, your spirit appears as a ghost at a nearby graveyard. All zones have at least one graveyard where dead characters reappear.

At the graveyard is a spirit healer. When you are a ghost, you can come back to life by retrieving your corpse or by asking the spirit healer to resurrect you. If you ask the ghost healer to resurrect you, you will lose a significant portion of experience. This amount will never force you to lose a level, however. If you do not wish to be raised immediately, then you must run to your corpse and recover it. It is almost always better to run to your corpse rather than ask a spirit healer to resurrect you. That's because all you lose when you run to your corpse is time. Aside from this slight inconvenience, there are no other penalties associated with dying and retrieving your corpse. Most zones have multiple graveyards interspersed around the zone so you likely won't be too far from your corpse anyway.

Corpse Retrieval

While you are a ghost, you run at increased speed. When you get close to your corpse, a resurrection window appears on your screen. To resurrect yourself, press the Resurrect Now button in the window. Be very careful about where you revive yourself. If you died fighting monsters, make sure the monsters are gone. When you raise yourself from the dead, your new body will replace your ghost, and you will appear with your health and mana bars half full.

Resurrection Waiting Period

If you have died repeatedly over a short period of time, subsequent resurrections might have a waiting period of a few minutes before you can return to life. However, this waiting period resets to zero if you then play for an extended period without dying. There is no resurrection waiting period if you are resurrected by the spell of another player.

Resurrection Spells

You can also be brought back from the dead through magic. Certain character classes can cast spells to raise you from the dead. The priest, shaman, and paladin all have resurrection spells. The difference between the resurrection spells of these casters is that they bring you back at different strengths. None of these classes begin play with their resurrection spells available, so it is an option that only higher-level characters can accommodate. When one of these classes casts a resurrection spell on you, you will be asked to consent to the resurrection. If you agree, you appear next to the caster with minimal health and mana as dictated by the spell.

Resurrection Sickness

When you are resurrected by a spell or soulstone, you revive with a condition called resurrection sickness. It lasts for a few minutes. During this time, all your character attributes are severely reduced and your maximum health and mana are much lower than normal. After the resurrection sickness passes, your attributes, health, and mana are restored to their normal numbers.

Resurrecting a Ghost

Even if you have already released your spirit and are now a ghost running back to your corpse, you can still benefit from a resurrection spell. In this case, you will get the same resurrection window asking you to consent to the resurrection. If you agree, you will appear near the casting shaman, priest, or paladin in your newly revived body.

Chapter 4

Advanced User Interface

This chapter provides additional details and advanced user options for your interface beyond the beginning information provided in Chapter 3: Getting Started.

CHARACTER SELECTION SCREEN

At the Character Selection screen you can make a new character, choose a character to play, change your current realm, enter the WoW website, access tech support, and adjust your account settings.

Create New Character Clicking the Create New Character button takes you to the character creation screen, where you can generate a character to play in the game. Chapter 3: Getting Started walks you through the character creation process. For detailed information on races and classes, see Chapter 6: Races and Classes.

The right side of the Character Selection screen lists any characters you have created. If you haven't yet made any characters, this area is blank. You can have up to ten characters per realm.

Each character entry shows the character's name, level, current location, and rest state. For more on the rest state, refer to Chapter 5: Your Character. Clicking on a character displays it in the center of your screen.

Delete Character To delete a character, select that character and then press the Delete Character button. You will be prompted to confirm the deletion. Click the Okay button to permanently erase that character.

Change Realm Realms are discrete game worlds. You can interact with all the players in your realm, but not with players in other realms. When you first play World of Warcraft, your realm will be pre-selected for you.

If you wish to play in a different realm, press the Change Realm button. A list appears showing all available realms and the current number of players in each realm. Click on the realm you want to join, and press the Okay button.

INTERFACE

Understanding Your Target

As you adventure in World of Warcraft, you will encounter more than just friendly NPCs and simple beasts. You will meet many creatures and characters, and you will need to understand how to interpret the information you get when viewing them.

FRIENDLY PLAYERS

Other friendly players appear with blue names over their heads, whether you have them selected or not. If they belong to a guild, their guild name will appear under their name. When you mouse over or select a friendly player, its tool tip will also appear blue.

OPPOSING PLAYERS

By default, all player characters have blue names. However, if a player turns on the player versus player flag and indicates that he or she wants to fight other players, then that player's name and tool tip turn red, indicating that they are hostile.

NON-PLAYER CHARACTERS (NPCs)

NPCs are any humanoid character you can interact with, such as merchants, aerial mount masters, and quest givers. Their names only appear over their heads when you click on them. The tool tips of friendly NPCs are green. The tool tips of enemy faction NPCs are red.

MONSTERS

Monsters are any characters that are not also faction's NPCs and that will fight back if you attack them. There are two categories of monsters: passive and aggressive. Passive monsters have yellow names and tool tips and only fight if struck first. Aggressive monsters have red names and tool tips, and attack you on sight. Some monsters are also social, and will call for help from others if they are in combat.

CRITTERS

Critters are non-combative animals, such as sheep, rabbits, cows, and prairie dogs. These animals will never fight you, even if you attack them. Killing a critter earns you no experience.

Additional Portraits

PET PORTRAIT

Some character classes can summon pets. If such a character is currently controlling a pet, a pet portrait appears underneath the main character portrait. The pet portrait displays the pet's name, health bar, and energy, mana, or rage bar. You can mouse over the bars for exact numbers.

PARTY MEMBER PORTRAITS

If you are grouped with other players, their portraits appear under yours as well. If you also have a pet, the party member portraits appear under your pet portrait. Each party member portrait displays the character's name, health bar, and energy, mana, or rage bar. Mousing over the party member's portrait also reveals its level and class, as well as any spell effects that are currently affecting the selected party member.

Spell and Ability Icons

Any beneficial spell or ability affecting your character appears in the upper right area of your map as an icon. You can mouse over the icon to see the buff's effect and duration. You can prematurely end any buff by right-clicking on its icon here.

Minimap

Simple geographical features, like rivers, mountains, and towns, are shown on your minimap. If you are near a town, its direction is indicated as a white arrow at the edge of your minimap.

If you have a pet or are grouped with another player, then this pet or player is shown on your minimap as a large green dot. If a party member is outside the radius of your minimap, then a yellow arrow at the edge of the minimap shows you his or her direction.

Whenever you use an ability that finds resources, such as find herbs or find minerals, then any applicable resources that are sufficiently nearby appear on your minimap as yellow dots. When you mouse over one of these dots, you see the name of whatever resource it represents. If the resource's name is grayed out, then that particular resource node is underground.

You can zoom the minimap in or out by pressing the plus and minus arrows on the edge of the minimap.

You can close the minimap by clicking the x above it. This closes the map, but not the name of the area.

Chat Log

In addition to chat messages from players in your immediate surroundings, the chat log also displays private messages from other players, guild messages, yells from other players, and any non-chat messages relating to your character development, such as notices for when you gain a level, earn a skill point, or acquire a quest. Only the last eight lines of messages are displayed, although you can scroll the log up to view previous messages. To jump back to the latest message, click on the bottom arrow key next to the chat log.

CHAT BUTTON

The chat button is especially important because it houses all the commands for effectively communicating with other players in World of Warcraft. By clicking on this button, you have access to party and guild chats, private messaging of individual players, emotes, and voiced speech. Many of these same chat options are also available through hotkeys or commands that you can type at the chat prompt.

CHAT PROMPT

The chat prompt appears below the chat log when you press the Enter key. At the chat prompt, you type the messages you want to say to your fellow players. Chat commands, such as yelling and whispering, can also be typed at the chat prompt instead of selected through the chat button.

For more information about chatting and using the special chat commands, refer to Chapter 10: Community, which tells you how to interact with other players in the World of Warcraft.

Combat Log

The combat log displays your actions and the actions of other nearby players, NPCs, and creatures. Combat, purchases, item creation, experience awards, or other activities are recorded in this combat log. The actions of monsters and other players appear in different colors to distinguish them from your actions.

The arrow keys to the right of the combat log let you scroll up and down the log to see previous actions. To jump back to the latest action, click on the bottom arrow key.

Action Bar

At the bottom of the screen is your action bar: the toolbar where you can store frequently used actions for quick and easy access. You can place abilities or inventory items in your action bar and then use them with the click of a mouse or the press of a key. For example, instead of opening your inventory bag and clicking on a hunk of bread to replenish your health, you can just click the hunk of bread icon on your action bar.

There are 12 slots on your action bar, and each can hold one spell, ability, or usable inventory item. Each action icon also has a hotkey – displayed in the icon's upper left corner – that corresponds to the 1 through 0 keys and the – and + keys on your keyboard. You can perform the action in an action slot by clicking on the icon there or by pressing the hotkey on your keyboard.

POPULATING YOUR ACTION BAR

To place an action in a slot on your action bar, open the window where the action appears (such as your Spellbook or backpack), left-click and drag (or or shift-left-click) the icon of the action to one of the 12 slots on the bar. To remove the command from your action bar, pick the action icon up by left-clicking on the icon in the action bar and then click on an empty area of your screen. This dumps the icon from your bar, although the action still remains in your Spellbook & Abilities panel or your inventory.

Holding your mouse over an action slot tells you what the action in that slot is.

NAVIGATING YOUR ACTION BARS

There are six action bars, but only one can be displayed at a time. You can navigate through the six action bars in three ways.

♦ You can scroll up or down your action bars by pressing the up and down arrows to the right of the action bar.

♦ You can jump to an action bar by holding down the Shift key and pressing any number key from 1 to 6. That will take you to one of the six action bars.

♦ You can scroll through the action bars by holding down the Shift key and scrolling with your mouse wheel.

MACROS

Macros are a very advanced type of user option that allows you to create hotkey buttons for your action bar that duplicate text messages, actions, and spellcasting. You could, for instance, bind the phrase "Hello everyone" to a single button using macros so that whenever you wanted to greet your guildmates, you only had to press your macro button instead of retyping the phrase each time.

You can even bind spells and abilities to your macro, and add text to your casting. Some players bind a healing spell, for example, and a phrase such as "I am healing %t [targeted player name]" to a single button.

Macros can save you a lot of time by automating some of your more common and repeated actions in the game.

CREATING A MACRO

To create a macro, open your chat prompt and type /macro.

Once you do that, a macro window pops up. To create a macro press the New button, type a name for your macro, and then select an icon for your macro and click the Okay button.

Next, in the macro text box, type the command you want to automate. When you are finished, you then drag the icon corresponding to this macro to an available slot on your action bar. The next time you want to execute the macro, you can just click on the macro icon on your action bar or press the appropriate hotkey.

For more detailed instructions on how to create and use macros, read the World of Warcraft strategy site at **http://www.worldofwarcraft.com** and look for game information. You can also type /macrohelp at the chat prompt for in-game instructions.

Pet Action Bar

If your character has access to a combat pet as a class feature, then anytime you summon a pet, a smaller action bar appears above your own. This pet action bar is used and populated the same way as your regular action bar. The hotkey for pet action bar icons is ctrl plus the appropriate number key. For example, the hotkey combination for your pet's first action bar icon is ctrl+1.

INTERFACE PANEL

The interface panel is the line of buttons at the bottom of your screen to the right of your action bar. By pressing on the individual buttons, you can view your character, open your spells and abilities book, select your character's talents, access your quests, interact with other players, see the world map, adjust game options, and get help. If you hold your mouse over each tab in the interface panel, you can see the name of the panel and its corresponding hotkey.

Character Info

The first button on the interface panel is Character Info. Clicking on this panel opens a window that shows your character and any equipment it is currently wearing. In addition to equipping yourself with items, you can also see the attributes, skills, and reputation of your character. This panel is explained in great detail in Chapter 5: Your Character.

Spellbook & Abilities

Clicking on the Spellbook & Abilities tab opens a book containing all the spells and abilities your character has. Most spells and abilities are acquired by purchasing them from a trainer, but some are only available as quest rewards. Any spell or ability you acquire shows up here once you pay for it. Holding your mouse over a spell or ability in the book tells you what that spell or ability does, how often you can cast it, and how much energy, mana, or rage it costs to use.

To use a spell or ability, you can open this book and then right-click or left-click on it to activate it. However, a much easier way to use an ability or spell is to add it to your action bar.

Your spells and abilities are kept in two separate sections. To switch between sections, press the appropriate tab at the bottom of the book. If you have more spells or abilities than can fit on one page, you can scroll to successive pages by clicking the left and right arrows at the bottom of the book.

If you have a combat pet, you will have a third tab on the bottom of your book with your pet's abilities.

In addition to class abilities and spells, the Spellbook & Abilities panel also is where trade skill abilities show up. The associated ability of a trade skill, such as the find herbs ability you get when you learn herbalism, appears in the Abilities section of your Spellbook & Abilities panel. You can drag such trade skill abilities to your action bar and use them as you would class abilities.

Talents

 The Talents button opens up your character's Talent window. Talents are additional powers you can select for your character that not only improve your existing abilities and spells, but that also customize your character. Using talents, two players of the same class can differentiate their characters greatly.

More information on talents can be found in Chapter 5: Your Character. The World of Warcraft online strategy guide at **http://www.worldofwarcraft.com** is your best source for up to date Talent information.

Quest Log

Whenever you acquire a quest, that quest is added to your quest log. All your currently active quests appear here.

The Quest Log window is organized into two sections: the quest list and the quest information window. The quest list shows all the quests you currently have, organized by the zone in which you acquired the quest. A zone only appears if you have a quest from there.

When you select a quest from the list, the quest info window displays all the information you need to complete it. The summary gives you the bare essentials for the quest: the goal you must achieve and the NPC you must talk to in order to complete the quest. Below the summary is the same text you received when you first acquired the quest, including the exact instructions and location of the quest, and any additional information you received at the time you acquired it. At the bottom of the quest info window is the reward heading, which tells you what you get if you complete the quest. Keep in mind that not all quests specify their possible rewards, and some quests unlock other quests.

When you complete a quest, it disappears from your quest log.

Your quest log can hold a maximum of 20 quests at a time. If you try to acquire a new quest, you get a message telling you your quest log is full. If that happens, you can complete a current quest to free up room to take on another quest, or abandon a current quest.

The quest log is explained in greater detail in Chapter 10: Adventuring.

Social

The Social window is where you keep track of your friends in the game, search for specific players, and display lists of players in the game by level, zone, name, or class. The four different sections of the Social window are: Friends, Ignore, Who, and Guild. You can switch between sections by clicking on the tabs at the bottom of the window. For more information on the Social window, refer to Chapter 10: Community.

FRIENDS

You can add people you enjoy playing with to the list in your Friends section. You can then refer to your friends list to see which friends are logged on and where they are playing. You are also notified when your friends log on or off.

IGNORE

The Ignore section is where you list players you wish to prevent from interacting or communicating with you.

WHO

This section is used to search for groups of players using key words, such as guild names, character classes, and races.

GUILD

The guild section is only available if you are a guild member. This section allows you to manage your guild relationships. It displays all members of your guild, whether they are online or offline, and shows their basic character information. If you are not a member of a guild, this tab is grayed out.

World Map

The World Map tab opens up a full-screen map of the world. The world map defaults to a hand-drawn map of your current zone. Any locations you have explored appear on the hand-drawn map. As you continue exploring, more locations will be drawn onto your map.

Your character appears as a yellow dot on the world map. If you are grouped, party members also appear as yellow dots. To tell who each yellow dot is, hold your mouse over the dot. The character's name will then pop up on your mouse cursor.

Major cities, such as the capitals for the eight playable races, already appear on your world map, even if you haven't explored them yet. Major cities that are not capitals also appear on the map.

To zoom out to a view of your continent, right-click on the map. Right-click again to zoom out for a map of the world. You can also adjust the view by clicking on the Zoom Out button at the top of the map.

The name of the zone or continent you are viewing is always displayed at the top of the world map. If you mouse over an explored location or known landmark, such as a city or mountain range, its name will appear at the top of the map instead.

You can also jump to a map of a specific zone by selecting a zone from the zone pulldown menu at the top of the screen. Left-click on the arrow next to the menu to open it, and then click on the desired zone. To jump to a different continent, press the arrow in the continent pulldown menu to the left. Jumping to a new continent will reset the zone pulldown menu to the zones in that continent.

Note

The world map covers your entire screen, blocking out your main window and the action bar. Be careful when opening the world map while you are in combat or running.

Help Request

The Help Request button opens up the suggestion, bug, and Game Master (GM) request menu. From here, you can report a bug, offer a suggestion for making the game better, or ask a GM for help. For more information on the Help Request panel, refer to Appendix IV: Customer Support.

Main Menu

Clicking on the Main Menu tab opens up the main menu. From here, you can adjust video and sound options, customize controls, logout, quit, or resume playing. You can also open the Main Menu by pressing the Escape key.

VIDEO AND SOUND OPTIONS

The Video Options button lets you control the detail you see in the game, as well as the resolution and brightness of the game. The Sound Options button lets you control the volume of music, ambient sounds, and character sounds in the game. Players with powerful systems should choose the highest settings for a richer experience, while players with less powerful systems should choose lower settings to increase game performance. To further enhance performance, certain settings, such as music volume or ambient sounds, can be disabled altogether.

INTERFACE OPTIONS

From this menu you can turn on more advanced options such as inverting the mouse, turning on the status bar (combat log), showing your pet melee and spell damage, turning on the right-click to move option, and more. More information on these advanced options can be found at the World of Warcraft strategy site at

http://www.worldofwarcraft.com

KEY BINDINGS

The Key Bindings menu lists all the hotkey commands in World of Warcraft and the default buttons associated with them. You can then customize all these hotkeys by typing in your own letters or mouse buttons. If you are later dissatisfied with your own key bindings, you can restore the Blizzard defaults.

LOGOUT AND QUIT

Clicking the Logout button takes you back to the Character Selection screen, while the Quit button closes World of Warcraft and takes you to the desktop.

CONTINUE

Pressing this button closes the main menu and takes you back to the game.

INTERACTING WITH THE WORLD AROUND YOU

Your mouse cursor is your primary means of interacting with the game world in World of Warcraft. It appears as a pointing gauntlet by default, which you can use to point at and then click on objects and characters in the game world. The keyboard is also used to complement the mouse in navigating around the world.

Smart Cursor

When your mouse cursor moves over an object or character that you can interact with, it sometimes changes shape to reflect a new action you can perform. It might turn into a bag if you mouse over a merchant, or a winged boot if you mouse over an aerial mount master. Experiment by visiting many NPCs and interacting with them.

Right-Clicking Versus Left-Clicking

If you want to select an object, creature, or character in World of Warcraft, left-click it. Left-clicking is also used if you want to select and drag items from your inventory bags or take spells and abilities from your Spellbook & Abilities panel to place in your action bar.

If you want to interact with an object or character, you must right-click it. Right-clicking will then perform an automatic command depending on the type of object or character you click on. For example, right-clicking a monster automatically begins an attack on it, right-clicking a resource node automatically makes you harvest it if you have the appropriate gathering trade skill. Right-clicking on other players opens up an interaction menu. If a target of a right-click has no possible interaction, then you will see an error message on your screen or your character will perform no action.

Click to Move

This option is turned on from the Interface Options menu. When this is turned on, right-clicking on an object, NPC, or monster automatically moves you to the necessary interactive distance to begin an interaction. If you are far away from a resource node and right-click on it, your character will run up to the node and then begin harvesting when you get in range. If you right-click on a quest giving NPC, you'll run up to the NPC and when you get within range, automatically pop open the NPC's dialog box and begin conversing.

You can also simply click on the ground to move to the location you select. The same principle applies to attacking monsters or using abilities on monsters. If you right-click on a monster, you run up to attack range.

The click to move functionality isn't just restricted to right-clicking. If you have a target selected and then perform an ability, whether through the action bar or your spells and abilities book, your character automatically moves to within range and uses the ability. Click to move is a useful option, but keep in mind that it also means your character will move automatically at the slightest right-click of the mouse.

Abilities That Require a Target

Some abilities require that you select a target after you click on them and before they occur. For example, for an Arcane Intellect spell, you would need to click on the Arcane Intellect icon on your action bar (or press the appropriate hotkey), then click on the target, and then your spell would be cast.

If this is the case, your hand cursor will glow, indicating that you must choose a target. A bright glow tells you that the target you are clicking on is legal. A dull glow indicates that you must find a new target.

Logging Out of the Game

To end your session in World of Warcraft, you can click on the Log Out or Quit buttons from the main menu. If you click on the Log Out button, a log out box appears in the middle of the screen. A 20-second timer in the log out box counts down to zero, at which point you are logged out of the game. To cancel your log out, press the cancel button. If you log out of the game while in an inn or one of the six capital cities, you log out immediately without a wait. When you click on the Quit button, you get a similar box and options. However, logging out takes you back to the Character Selections screen, while quitting closes the game and takes you to the desktop.

Chapter 5

Your Character

Your character has a variety of distinguishing features, such as attributes, skills, abilities, and talents, that come together to create a unique individual within the game.

Character Info Window

To view information about your character, click on the Character Info button at the bottom of the screen. Alternatively, you can press the hotkey C to open up this window.

Within this window, you can see your character, all equipment he is wearing, attributes, and secondary characteristics. Tabs at the bottom of the window can also be clicked to open up your character's reputation and skills pages.

Attributes

The basic building blocks for your character are your attributes. They determine your physical and mental aptitude.

The five attributes that define your character are listed below. They are primary attributes that influence secondary characteristics.

Strength: Strength determines the physical power of your character. A high strength improves your attack power. Strength is also a determining factor in how much damage you block if you use a shield. Rogues and hunters only use a partial value of strength to determine their power.

Agility: Agility improves your armor rating, your chance to dodge an attack, and your chance to score a critical hit with a melee or ranged attack, thus dealing increased damage. Rogues and hunters also use agility, in combination with strength, to determine their attack power.

Stamina: Stamina affects your hit points, no matter what class you play. However, characters designed to absorb damage, such as warriors and paladins, gain more benefit from stamina than classes who have other capabilities, such as rogues and druids, who in turn gain more benefit than pure spellcasters, such as mages.

Intelligence: Intelligence improves your mana reserves. Intelligence has no bearing on non-spellcasting classes.

Spirit: Spirit determines the regeneration rate for your health and mana. A high spirit results in much faster regeneration, while a low spirit gives you reduced regeneration.

Secondary Characteristics

Your secondary characteristics are stats that depend in some part on your class selection and your primary attributes. Such stats include your health, mana, energy, rage, attack, power, damage per second, defense, armor, and resistances.

Health: Health, also called hit points, represents how much damage your character can take before it dies. Health is set by your class, and increases as you level up. In addition, the stamina attribute gives you a bonus to your health. Each class gets a different number of bonus hit points for each stamina point they possess, with classes that are melee fighters getting the most increase due to stamina, and spellcasters getting the least. Your health is displayed as a green bar at the top of the screen next to your character portrait.

Mana: Mana is what you pay to cast your spells if your class has any spellcasting capability. These classes are mages, priests, warlocks, druids, shaman, paladins, and hunters. The spells of these classes have mana costs that must be paid in order to be cast. The amount of mana you have is set by your class, with primary spellcasters, like priests and mages, getting more than hybrid spellcasters, such as druids and shaman. Classes that are even less reliant on spells, such as hunters and paladins, have even less mana. In addition, your character's intellect gives you a bonus to mana. Each class gets a different amount of bonus mana, with primary spellcasters getting more for each point of intellect than other spellcasters. Your mana is displayed as a blue bar next to your character portrait.

Energy: Energy is used to power rogue abilities. Unlike mana or health, energy does not improve with level, nor is it influenced by any attribute. A rogue's energy bar always starts at 100 points, unless modified by a rogue talent. When a rogue uses a special attack or ability, it costs energy points. Energy replenishes fairly quickly over time, so a rogue can continue to perform special attacks during a battle. However, energy regeneration isn't rapid enough to allow a rogue to continue to use many abilities indefinitely. The rage bar is displayed in yellow underneath the character's health bar.

Rage: Rage is spent on the use of warrior abilities. Unlike mana or energy, rage does not begin as a full bar. It, like energy, is not influenced by an attribute. Rage has a limit of 100, but a warrior's rage bar always starts at zero. Your rage bar appears as an empty bar under your health. As it fills up, it turns red.

Attack: Attack, also called attack rating, increases your chances of hitting a target in battle with your weapon. It is directly tied to your weapon skill with your current weapon.

Power: Power, also called attack power, increases the damage you do with your weapons. All classes have a base attack power. Classes geared towards combat have higher base power than classes that are geared towards spellcasting. Strength is added to power as a bonus, resulting in greater attack power for stronger characters.

Damage: Damage depends on the weapon you use and on your power. All weapons have a damage rating. When you equip the weapon, the damage of your character includes the weapon's damage, plus bonuses from your power and class. Spells and abilities can temporarily boost damage. Damage-per-second, or DPS, is shown as tool tip info.

Defense: Defense reduces your chance of being hit in combat by physical blows. It is directly tied to your defense class skill.

Armor: Armor reduces the amount of damage you take from physical blows. Armor is actually made up of your agility, plus the armor rating of any armor you have equipped. Based on your armor rating and type of armor, you have a chance to reduce the damage you take from enemy attacks.

Resistances: Resistances give you a percentage chance to resist some or all of the damage or effects from spells. Resistances begin at zero, but can be improved with items and spells.

CHARACTER LEVELS

In World of Warcraft, your character level determines how powerful you are. Higher-level characters are stronger, more durable, and more deadly than lower-level characters. Higher-level characters can also accomplish more with their spells and abilities, and overcome much tougher obstacles and enemies.

All characters start at level one in the game, and can advance in level by earning experience. The level cap in the game is 60. Once you achieve level 60, you cannot gain any more levels. Keep in mind that as an online role-playing game, World of Warcraft is always being updated with extra content. While at its release, the game has a level cap of 60, this cap will increase in the future as the game continues to evolve.

Experience

Experience is the only means of advancing your character levels, and is gained in two primary ways. Most experience comes from defeating monsters and from completing quests. A third means of gaining experience – exploring the world – gives you so little experience compared to the two primary methods that it can't really help you gain character levels.

Experience from Monsters

Every time you kill a monster that is a challenge for your character, you earn experience. The more challenging the monster, the greater the experience reward. The weaker the monster, the less the reward.

KOBOLD EXCAVATION CREW

Trivial Monsters

You are able to tell which monsters are trivial because their level will appear gray in their target portrait.

You do not gain experience for killing monsters that are so far below your level that they pose no challenge. This threshold changes depending on your level. At low levels, you gain no experience from killing monsters more than five levels lower than you. This minimum level threshold grows slightly for higher-level characters, though, so that high-level characters have more leeway in the kills they can make and earn experience for.

"You no take candle!"

Quest Experience

When you turn in a completed quest, you gain an experience reward. This quest reward is often substantial, and equal to several, if not a dozen, monster kills at once. Quests will range in difficulty, so the rewards will also vary.

Doing quests is an extremely efficient way to earn experience and gain levels. Players who only kill monsters do not typically level as quickly as those who also complete quests. Furthermore, not only do quests help you level more quickly, but they also carry material rewards as well.

The Experience Bar

Stretching across the bottom of your screen is your experience bar. At the beginning of a level, it is empty, but as you earn experience, it begins to fill. You can mouse over the experience bar to see your current experience, and the amount you need for next level. When it fills up completely, you gain a new level, and the experience bar resets to zero.

In addition, the amount of experience you need for the next level increases an incremental amount. Leveling up becomes progressively harder, not only because your challenges are greater at higher levels, but also because the experience requirement grows.

Rest State

In World of Warcraft, the rest state has a great effect on how much experience you earn from kills. When your character is rested, they earn 200 percent of the experience from a kill. However,

rest state is a temporary condition, and you become less rested after you accumulate a certain amount of experience through encounters.

All characters begin the game in a normal state. Rest state can only be accumulated when your character is standing in an inn, logged out from an inn, or logged out from the wilderness. While you are in an inn or logged out from an inn, your rest state increases every few hours. If you log out in the wilderness, your rest state accumulation is much slower. For the purposes of rest state accumulation, logging out in one of the six capital cities – Orgrimmar, Thunder Bluff, Undercity, Darnassus, Ironforge, and Stormwind – is the same as logging out from an inn.

Rest state grows slowly every hour you are logged out of the game or in an inn, but the longer you are away from the game, the greater your rest. There is a maximum amount of rest state you can amass, and that usually is enough to give you a 200 percent experience bonus for one and a half experience bars. However, in order to accumulate that much rest, you usually need to be logged out for more than a week.

Rest state is meant as a reward for those who are away from the game and then return. It's a way to jump back into the game and level quickly if you've been left behind while your friends all leveled during your absence. It is not meant as a continual reward for those who play as often as several hours a day.

Rest State Marker

A rest state marker exists on your experience bar to tell you how rested you are. When the filled portion of your experience bar hits the marker, your character then goes to a normal rest state. In this normal state, you earn 100 percent of experience from a kill, meaning you get no experience bonus. To regain your rest, you must then go to an inn or log out of the game. The rest state marker only appears on your experience bar when you are rested.

Rest State and Quests

Experience you earn from completing quests has no effect on your rest state. Nor does rest state give you a bonus to quest experience. Quest experience does not move you to the normal state any faster. Only monster experience is counted towards your loss of rest.

What It Means to Level

When you gain a level, your character becomes more powerful. Your attributes increase; you class skills increase; and as a result, many secondary characteristics, such as health and mana, improve as well. In addition, you gain the ability to purchase trade skills and talents, and to acquire to new abilities.

Attribute Increases

Primary attributes that are important to your class automatically increase by one or two points when you level up. These attribute increases will change from level to level, but spellcasters will usually gain intellect and spirit boosts, while melee fighters will often gain stamina and strength boosts. However, over the course of your character's full level range, you will get increases to most, if not all, attributes.

Secondary Characteristics

When you level, you also get an increase in health. If your character is a spellcaster or has spellcasting abilities, you also get an increase in mana. In addition, if your stamina and intellect increase when you level, you also get another boost to your health and mana through your attribute improvement.

Class Skills

Your class skills, which determine the effectiveness of your class spells and abilities, do not automatically improve when you level up. Instead, they improve as you use them. However, the skill cap you have in a class skill does increase when you gain a level. For example, as a first level priest, your maximum skill level in holy magic is five. As you cast holy spells, your holy skill will eventually max out at five points, until you advance to the next level and your holy magic skill cap increases.

Talents

Your talents are accessible from the Talents window, which can be opened by clicking on the Talents button at the bottom of the screen or by pressing the hotkey N. See chapter 7.

Spells and Abilities

Aside from attribute and stat increases, the other major way in which your character grows in power is through access to new spells and abilities.

Learning New Spells and Abilities

When your character increases in level, it is a good idea to return to your class trainer to learn new abilities. Class trainers exist in all major cities, but not every class will be represented. You won't find any shaman trainers in Alliance cities, for example, because the shaman is a Horde-only class. Even within a faction, trainers only exist where a large segment of the population can train in that class. Shaman trainers don't exist in the undead capital of Undercity because undead can't be shaman either.

You can always talk to your class trainer, no matter your level. The trainer then shows you a list of all spells and abilities you can learn in the training window.

All your spells and abilities are organized into different categories or schools. These categories mirror your class skills. Shaman, for example, have earth, fire, and water skills.

By browsing through the list of items, you can see all the spells and abilities to look forward to as you level. When you click on a spell or ability, a summary of it appears at the bottom of the window. You can also see the level requirement for the ability. If you mouse over the picture of the ability, an info box opens that reveals more detailed information.

Once you achieve a high enough level to learn a new spell or ability, return to your trainer, select a spell or ability, and click on the Train button at the bottom of the window to learn it.

Using Spells and Abilities

Once you acquire a new spell or ability, it is added to your Spellbook or Abilities book. You can then copy the spell or ability to your action bar for easier use. Passive abilities, which are always on, do not need to be attached to your action bar for use.

All spells and abilities that you use fall into several different categories.

Instant cast: Instant-cast spells or abilities can be used or cast instantaneously. You cannot be interrupted when using the spell or ability.

Timed cast: Timed-cast spells and abilities have a brief casting time. When you click on the spell or ability to use it, a casting meter appears at the bottom of your screen. When the meter fills, your spell is cast. You can be interrupted while casting the spell if you are hit or affected by an enemy's special attack. Each hit from an enemy resets your casting meter or pushes it back, delaying the time it takes you to use the spell or ability. An attack that completely interrupts your spell or ability, such as a stunning effect, will erase your entire casting meter. In this case, you must recast the spell or ability.

Channeled: Channeled spells only take effect as long as you continue casting them. When you channel a spell, a reversed casting meter appears at the bottom of your screen. It begins full, and as you channel the spell, the meter dwindles. When the meter is depleted, the spell ends. While you are channeling the spell, the target suffers or benefits from the effect, which usually occurs every few seconds. If you move while channeling a spell or you are affected by an interrupting effect, the channeled spell ends. If you are hit in combat, the channeling bar will deplete further, but without an increase in the channeled spell's effect. In other words, being hit in combat while you are casting a channeled spell causes the casting time and effects of your spell to be decreased.

Passive: Passive abilities are always on. They do not need to be cast and cannot be used through the action bar. As soon as you learn them, they are in constant effect. Some examples of passive abilities are dodge and block.

Spell and Ability Delays

Spells and abilities can't always be cast or used repeatedly. Instead, many of them have a brief delay you must observe before you can cast or use the ability again. After you use a spell or ability, its icon on the action bar and Spells and Abilities book darkens. When it brightens again, you can use it once more. This delay is often called the spell or ability's cooldown time by players.

EQUIPMENT

Although much of your character's power comes from your attributes and abilities, the equipment you wear is just as important to your growth.

In many cases, your equipment can improve your character dramatically by giving you a great DPS boost, enhancing your attributes, improving your armor and defense, or boosting your spell power and resistances.

On the Character Info window, there are equipment slots on either side of your character model. These equipment slots correspond to different parts of your character's body. The slots on the side are for armor and jewelry. The four slots at the bottom are for your hand-held equipment, which can include melee weapons, ranged weapons, shields, ammunition, wands, and miscellaneous objects.

ARMOR SLOTS

The different body parts on which you can equip armor are your head, shoulders, back, chest, wrists, hands, waist, legs, and feet. You can have one piece of armor per slot.

Of these armor types, the ones that are easiest to acquire, and thus available at early levels, are back, chest, wrists, hands, waist, legs, and feet armor. Later you begin to find rings and shoulder armor. At mid-levels you find necklaces and helmets. At higher levels you find trinkets.

SHIRT SLOT

Your character has a slot to wear a shirt. However, shirts are usually decorative and have no in-game benefits. They can, however, make you stand out among your fellow players. Tailors can make a variety of different colored shirts, and you can also find shirts as quest rewards or treasure.

TABARD SLOT

One slot on the left is for a tabard, which is a vestment with your guild crest. You can purchase a tabard even if you are not in a guild. If you do, it will appear as a plain gray tabard. It will acquire your guild insignia when your guild chooses a design or when you join a guild that already has a design.

JEWELRY

There are two slots for a character to wear rings. Rings are rare magic items that you can win as quest rewards or find as drops from monsters. There is a wide variety of rings. Some improve attributes and statistics, while others give you the ability to heal or do spell damage. Rings do not show up on your character when you wear them, although they are equipped.

Necklaces are similar to rings, but there is only one necklace slot.

Trinket's are even rarer than rings and necklaces. They do not show up on your character, but can confer a wide range of abilities on you." Trinkets do not have the same qualities. They are usually right-click effect items.

HAND-HELD EQUIPMENT

The four slots at the bottom of your character window are for your hand-held equipment. The first slot is for your primary hand; the second slot is for your offhand; the third slot is for your ranged weapon; and the fourth slot is for your ammunition.

MELEE WEAPONS

If you wield a one-handed weapon, it must be placed in your primary hand to be effective. If you wield a two-handed weapon, it is placed in your primary hand slot, but also occupies your offhand slot.

Your offhand slot can accommodate a secondary weapon if you have the dual wield class skill. It can also hold an offhand item, such as a shield, torch, orb, magic branch, or lantern. If you are wielding a two-handed weapon, your offhand slot is already occupied.

RANGED WEAPONS

Your ranged slot can hold a ranged weapon appropriate for your character, whether that is a wand, bow, gun, or thrown projectile. You can have a ranged weapon equipped here, at the same time that you have a melee weapon equipped in your primary and offhand slots.

To ready a ranged weapon for use, open your Ability book. If you have an equipped ranged weapon, a shoot ability should appear in your book. You can shoot your ranged weapon by clicking the shoot ability in the book, or drag the shoot icon to your action bar to use. Any time you need to use your ranged weapon, you can press this button and fire away. Your character will pull out the ranged weapon and attack. Unlike melee attacks, ranged attacks cannot be toggled on or off. You need to press the shoot button each time you want to attack.

AMMO SLOT

Guns and bows require ammunition to use. In this case, you need to place ammunition, bullets or arrows, in the ammo slot. As long as you have ammo of the appropriate type in your inventory, you can fire your weapon.

Equipment Level Requirements

Much of the equipment you make or find has a level requirement. If you mouse over a piece of equipment, at the bottom of the item's info box is level requirement, telling you the minimum level you have to have in order to use the item. Some items, such as armor and weapons you acquire as quest rewards, do not have a level requirement. If you can complete the quest, then you deserve to use the armor or weapon, regardless of your level.

Some items also require a trade skill to use. For instance, most items created by engineers require some level of engineering skill to equip or use.

Consumable items, such as potions, also have level requirements, even when they are quest rewards. If you are not yet high enough level to equip or use an item, the level requirement in the info box appears red to you.

Unusable Equipment

Equipment that you cannot use usually shows up as red to you. For instance, if you are browsing a weapon merchant's wares, any weapons you cannot use because of your class will appear red in the merchant window.

If you mouse over a weapon in your inventory that you cannot use because of a single condition, then that condition is in red text. If you aren't high enough level to wear the item, then the level requirement text in the info box is red. If you don't yet have the appropriate weapon skill, then the weapon type is in red letters.

Unusable equipment cannot be equipped by your character.

Soulbound Equipment

Many of the most powerful items and equipment in the game are soulbound. Soulbound items cannot be traded to other players. They can be sold to a vendor, stored in the bank, or destroyed. You cannot auction off a soulbound item at an auction house. If an item is soulbound, then it will say so just under the item's name in its info box. Items have different conditions for becoming soulbound. These options are as follows:

Bind on acquire: This item is bound to you as soon as you pick it up from a corpse or quest giver. Most quest rewards bind on pickup.

Bind on equip: This item is bound as soon as you place it in an equipment slot. Once it is equipped, the item is soulbound and cannot trade hands again. Most good items that are made through trade skills bind on equip.

Bind on use: This item is bound as soon as you use it. Such items are generally not able to be equipped but have an effect that you use directly from your inventory. Most items that summon mounts are bind on use.

Quest items: Quest items are a special category of soulbound item. If you are looking for items in order to fulfill a quest, these items often have the quest item tag where the soulbound tag usually appears. Items with the quest item tag cannot be traded to other players or sold to NPC vendors.

Equipment Rarity

Many of the items and equipment you find in the world fall into different categories of rarity; this category in turn tells you how weak or powerful these items are. The rarer the item is, the more fantastic its properties.

You can tell the rarity, and thus potency, of items by the color of their name. This color appears the same whether you mouse over the item to see its name in an info box, whether you see it linked in chat, or whether you see it as a message when it is picked up in a group.

Gray: These items are of poor quality and have no special properties. They are often called vendor trash by players.

White: These items are of common quality. Usually, only high-level white items have special properties. Most vendor-bought items fall into this category.

Green: Rarer than white items and often more powerful, these items are considered uncommon. Green items can be disenchanted with the enchanting trade skill for magic reagents useful in enchanting other equipment. Green items are mostly found as loot or created by trade skill craftspeople.

Blue: Blue items are of rare quality, and almost always have special properties. They are also considered magical for the purposes of the enchanting skill. Only a handful of items a craftsperson can make are blue items, and even then, such items require many obscure ingredients to craft and can only be made by craftspeople with a high skill level.

Purple: These items are epic in scope and power.

It is rumored that even more powerful items exist in the world...

Armor Sets

Rumors persist of unique, distinguished item sets that once belonged to great heroes and legends. These sets are said to bestow additional magic abilities once all their pieces have been found and equipped. When a character is equipped with all the items of a set, additional bonus magic attributes are added as well. When a set item is selected, the names of all the items in the set are listed on the tool tip

Durability

As weapons and armor get used, they start to wear down. Eventually, armor that continues to get battered in combat will begin to degrade in quality, as will weapons that keep biting into the tough hide of monsters.

In World of Warcraft, every time you use a weapon or suffer a blow in battle, your weapon or armor has a chance to take a hit in durability.

Your equipment's current durability can be seen by mousing over it from your Character Info window or your inventory. When a piece of equipment drops to low durability, you will see a small representation of your character and the damaged equipment in the corner of your screen.

When a piece of equipment's durability gets very low, you can repair it at a merchant NPC who specializes in working on the particular item that requires attention.

If an item drops to zero durability, it become useless and will no longer confer any benefits to your character. It will remain equipped on your character, but armor will cease to provide protection and weapons will be so worn down that you will effectively attack as if you had no weapon.

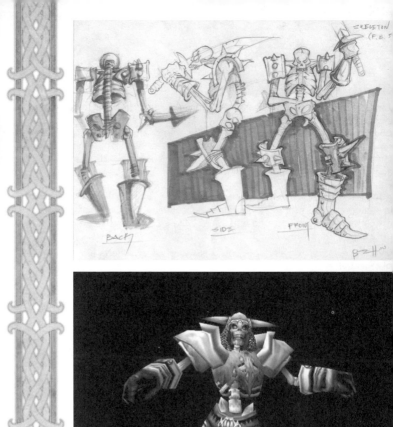

Inventory

As you adventure through the world, you find treasure and items. All this loot gets put in your inventory, or bag slots. In the lower right portion of your screen is your backpack, which you start with, and four empty slots to the left. These empty slots can accommodate a bag each. Bags come in different varieties, and can be found by a variety of means. You can buy them from vendors or players, get them as loot or reward, or make them yourself with tailoring.

Your default backpack is a 16-slot container, and it can thus hold sixteen items – one in each slot. New bags you acquire can be as small as 4-slot containers, or bigger than your backpack. When you find a new bag, it is placed in an existing slot in your backpack or existing bag. To equip a new bag and enable it as a container, you must place it in an empty bag slot by dragging it there. It can then begin holding items.

Opening & Closing Bags

To open a bag, you can click on it or press the appropriate hotkey. The hotkey for the backpack is F12 or B, and from right to left, the hotkeys for the other four bags are F11, F10, F9, and F8. To open all bags at once, press the Shift-B.

Interacting with Items in Your Bags

To interact with an item, open your bag. Left-clicking the item picks it up. Right-clicking the item equips it if the item can be equipped or uses the item if it has an effect but cannot be equipped. Mousing over the item pops up an info box with information on the item.

Quivers & Ammo Pouches

Quivers and ammo pouches are another type of container that can be equipped in a bag slot. These items can only hold ammunition of the appropriate type. They generally have more slots than normal containers as well as improving combat with a ranged weapon.

Chapter 6
Races and Classes

There are eight playable races in World of Warcraft, divided between the two factions of Horde and Alliance. When you choose your race, you also are choosing your potential classes, starting area, and racial capital. Your starting area and racial capital only serve as your introduction into the game world. All players are free to travel as far as their abilities take them, although great dangers from the environment and even other players await you in unfriendly lands.

Each race, in addition to its class selection, has unique racial traits. Some abilities are innate, but not all abilities are available at the beginning of play. Some only become learnable after you achieve a certain level, and others must be learned as talents. In rare cases, a race might have to successfully complete a quest to unlock a racial ability. Potential racial abilities can be seen at the Character Selection screen when you click on the appropriate race.

There are nine available classes in World of Warcraft. Many share certain traits and can be grouped into general categories. However, all have their unique strengths and abilities.

The Alliance

Dwarf
Class Selection: Hunter, Mage, Rogue, Paladin, Priest, Warrior
Starting Area: Coldridge Valley, Dun Morogh
Capital City: Ironforge

Gnome
Class Selection: Mage, Rogue, Warlock, Warrior
Starting Area: Coldridge Valley, Dun Morogh
Capital City: Ironforge

Human
Class Selection: Mage, Priest, Paladin, Rogue, Warlock, Warrior
Starting Area: Northshire Valley, Elwynn Forest
Capital City: Stormwind

Night Elf
Class Selection: Druid, Hunter, Rogue, Priest, Warrior
Starting Area: Shadowglen, Teldrassil
Capital City: Darnassus

The Horde

Orc
Class Selection: Hunter, Rogue, Shaman, Warlock, Warrior
Starting Area: Valley of Trials, Durotar
Capital City: Orgrimmar

Tauren
Class Selection: Druid, Hunter, Shaman, Warrior
Starting Area: Camp Narache, Mulgore
Capital City: Thunder Bluff

Troll
Class Selection: Hunter, Mage, Rogue, Priest, Shaman, Warrior
Starting Area: Valley of Trials, Durotar
Capital City: Orgrimmar

Undead
Class Selection: Mage, Priest, Rogue, Warlock, Warrior
Starting Area: Deathknell, Tirisfal Glades
Capital City: Undercity

The Warrior

The warrior is the toughest of all classes in World of Warcraft. They have the highest health of any class, can use the best weapons, can wear the heaviest armor, and can also deal an excellent amount of damage. Melee combat is the warriors' forte, and while they aren't as quick or lethal as the rogue, nor as adept at ranged combat as the mage or hunter, they are nevertheless one of the toughest classes in World of Warcraft.

Allowable Races: All

Primary Attributes: Stamina, Strength

Common Weapon Skills: One-Handed Axes, Daggers, One-Handed Maces, One-Handed Swords, Unarmed

Advanced Weapon Skills: Crossbows, Fist weapons, Bows or Guns, Polearms, Spears, Staves, Thrown, Two-Handed Axes, Two-Handed Maces, Two-Handed Swords

Armor Proficiencies: Cloth, Leather, Mail, Shield, Plate (Advanced)

Class Abilities

Warriors, in addition to their wide weapon and armor options, have a host of combat abilities that make them tough to kill and strong in melee combat.

Warrior abilities are divided into the categories of protection, arms, and fury. These abilities include passive defenses, special attacks, and shouts that affect the warrior, its allies, and its enemies. Those abilities that are not passive require rage to use.

Stances

Most abilities can only be used when the warrior is in a certain stance. There are several different stances a warrior can learn. The initial stance for a warrior is the battle stance. Battle stance abilities include offensive and defensive powers. As the warrior levels, it gains access to its defensive stance and berserker stance by completing warrior-only quests.

Defensive stance abilities improve the warrior's ability to stand toe-to-toe with opponents. It is the stance of choice for warriors who wish to increase their durability in combat at the expense of offense. Berserker stance abilities are nearly all offensive. In this stance, the warrior isn't as effective at diverting the attacks of enemies, but is more capable of killing monsters quickly.

Switching to a different stance brings up a new set of action bars that you must populate with the relevant stance abilities.

SAMPLE WARRIOR ABILITIES

This is a small sample of abilities available to the warrior. More fantastic abilities are available at even higher levels.

 Battle Shout: Boosts the attack power of the warrior and any nearby party members. Higher ranks increase attack power further.

 Charge: The warrior rushes the enemy, generating rage for the warrior. Requires battle stance. Higher ranks can stun the target.

 Hamstring: Does damage to the enemy and slows its movement speed greatly. Higher ranks do more damage. Requires battle stance.

 Taunt: Forces nearby enemies to disengage from their current target and attack the warrior. Higher ranks are more effective. Requires defensive stance.

 Disarm: Disarms the target's weapon for a short duration, forcing it to fight unarmed. Requires defensive stance.

 Cleave: Does massive damage to a target and a nearby enemy. Requires berserker stance.

 Recklessness: Turns all your attacks into critical hits for a few seconds and makes you immune to fear, but greatly lowers your armor. Requires battle stance.

Rage

Rage is built up when a warrior takes damage, uses certain abilities, or damages an enemy. When the warrior's rage bar begins to fill with rage, the warrior can then execute special attacks or abilities that cost rage. Rage dissipates quickly over time, although certain warrior abilities and talents can delay this eventual dissipation.

The Mage

The mage is a master of powerful mystic energies, able to use magic in the most spectacular and destructive of ways. Mages are a fragile class, with little health and poor fighting ability. However, they make up for this physical weakness with their awesome spellcasting. Mages can dish out the most ranged damage in the shortest time.

Allowable Races: Human, Gnome, Dwarf, Troll, Undead

Primary Attributes: Intellect, Spirit

Common Weapon Skills: Staves, Unarmed, Wands

Advanced Weapon Skills: Daggers, One-Handed Swords

Armor Proficiencies: Cloth

Class Abilities

The mage is the master of powerful offensive magic and has a host of other unique abilities. They exist to blast monsters from range. In fact, in this role, they are unrivaled by all classes. Only the rogue can hope to approach the massive amount of damage the mage can deal out, and even then, the rogue must get to within melee range to do so. Mage spells fall into three schools: arcane, frost, and fire. Their frost and fire spells are mostly offensive, although the frost school does have spells that can protect the mage and freeze or slow the mage's target. Arcane spells include some offensive and defensive spells, and non-combat spells such as teleport.

Mages have little capacity to defend themselves if they run out of mana. They have weak combat skills and low health. However, mages can summon food and drink to replenish their health and mana, and at much higher levels, they can create mana stones that can instantly restore mana, extending their effectiveness in combat.

SAMPLE MAGE SPELLS AND ABILITIES

This is a small sample of spells available to the mage. More fantastic spells are available at even higher levels.

 Arcane Intellect: Boosts the mage's intellect for a limited duration. Higher ranks give a higher intellect boost.

 Blizzard: Calls down ice shards over a wide area, doing massive damage to enemies. This is a channeled spell. Higher ranks do more damage.

 Fireball: Shoots a long-range blast of fire at the target, doing damage and burning the target for a few seconds. Higher ranks do more damage.

 Frost Armor: Boosts the mage's armor, and also slows any enemies that hit the mage. Higher ranks add more armor.

 Frost Nova: Blasts all enemies in the area with cold damage, and roots them in place for a few seconds. Higher ranks do more damage.

 Mana Shield: Creates a temporary shield that deducts hit point damage from the mage's mana instead of health. Higher ranks last longer and absorb more damage.

 Polymorph: Turns the target into a sheep. While polymorphed, the target wanders around and cannot attack, but it also regenerates health rapidly. Any damage to the target ends the spell prematurely.

The Priest

The priest is a spellcaster with a diverse portfolio of spells. This class has the most potent healing spells, as well as excellent buffs. It also has good defensive spells that can ward allies from physical dangers and spells, as well as purely offensive shadow spells. However, as a primary spellcaster, the priest is extremely fragile, with poor health and weak melee power.

Allowable Classes: Dwarf, Human, Night Elf, Troll, Undead

Primary Attributes: Intellect, Spirit

Common Weapon Skills: One-Handed Maces, Unarmed, Wands

Advanced Weapon Skills: Daggers, Staves

Armor Proficiencies: Cloth

Class Abilities

Priests are pure spellcasters whose strengths are healing and defensive spells. Priest spells are divided between the holy and shadow schools, and fall into several categories: heals, attack spells, crowd control, and buffs. While the shaman, druid, and paladin can also heal, none of them can heal as well as the priest. Also, the priest has better resurrection spells than the paladin or shaman.

Among a priest's best protection and buff spells are the holy word spells, which can absorb damage in battle and boost the stamina of the priest or its allies.

Another large class of spells the priest has is direct damage spells like mind blast, and damage-over-time spells like shadow word: pain. The priest also has good spells to counter enemy casters, such as mana burn.

SAMPLE PRIEST SPELLS

This is a small sample of spells available to the priest. More fantastic spells are available at even higher levels.

 Holy Smite: Blasts the target with a jolt of holy damage. Higher ranks do more damage.

 Holy Word: Fortitude: Temporarily increases the stamina of a friendly target. Higher ranks improve stamina further.

 Holy Word: Shield: Erects a shield over the target that absorbs some damage before it disappears. While shielded, a spellcaster cannot be interrupted from all damage spells. Higher ranks absorb more damage.

 Inner Fire: Greatly increases the priest's attack power and armor for a short duration. Higher ranks improve attack and armor further.

 Lesser Heal: A beginning healing spell that replenishes some health. Higher ranks heal more.

 Mana Burn: Drains a massive amount of mana from the target spellcaster, doing half that much in hit point damage as well to the target.

 Resurrection: Revives a dead player with minimal health and mana. Higher ranks bring the target back with more health and mana.

The Rogue

The rogue is one of the most lethal character classes in the game, able to deal out immense damage in a short period of time. The most effective rogues sneak through the shadows without detection, and then strike enemies from behind with a flurry of assassination attacks. Yet, for all their fast-hitting power, rogues are not very durable, relying on quickness and stealth for protection instead of armor and high health.

Allowable Races: Orc, Troll, Undead, Dwarf, Gnome, Human, Night Elf

Primary Attributes: Agility, Strength, Stamina

Common Weapon Skills: Daggers, Thrown, Unarmed

Advanced Weapon Skills: Bows, Crossbows, Fist Weapons, Guns, One-Handed Maces, One-Handed Swords

Armor Proficiencies: Cloth, Leather

Class Abilities

The rogue has an array of abilities. It can sneak past enemies undetected, deliver massive damage through special attacks, finishing moves and use poisons. The rogue can also learn lockpicking to open doors and chests, and learn the pick pockets ability to steal coins and items.

Many of the rogue's combat abilities require energy to use. Rogues begin combat with their energy bars filled, but lose energy as they use abilities. The bar refreshes quickly over time, though. Managing the energy bar is thus one of the rogue's primary responsibilities during combat.

In addition to dealing damage and achieving special effects, the rogue's combat abilities also generate combo points.

Combination Points

Combo points are only generated when the rogue uses certain special attacks or abilities. The rogue's powerful finishing moves require combo points to use, in addition to the normal energy expenditure. A rogue can accumulate a maximum of five combo points. You can see how many combo points you have by looking at the target monster's NPC portrait. The combo points appear as red dots.

When a finishing move is executed, all combo points are spent, and the move takes effect. A minimum of one combo point is required to use the finishing move, but the more combo points spent, the greater the effect.

SAMPLE ROGUE ABILITIES

This is a small sample of abilities available to the rogue. More fantastic abilities are available at even higher levels.

Backstab: The rogue's primary starting attack at early levels. Does greater damage to the enemy, although the rogue must be behind the target to attack.

Blind: Blinds target for several seconds, causing it to wander around in a confused state.

Expose Armor: Finishing move that reduces the target's armor. The more combo points spent, the greater the armor reduction. Higher ranks reduce armor further.

Eviscerate: Finishing move that does more damage the more combo points you have accumulated. Higher ranks do even more damage.

Gouge: Damages and disorients your target. If you attack the target before the disorientation wears off, the target automatically awakens. Awards one combo point.

Sap: Knocks out a humanoid target for an extended duration. The rogue must be stealthed to use this ability. Only works on humanoids out of combat. Any damage the target suffers wakes it up immediately. Only one target may be sapped at a time. Higher ranks stun the target longer.

Stealth: Places the rogue in stealth mode. Cannot be used in combat. While stealthed, the rogue turns transparent, and can sneak around enemies with a lower chance of being detected. If you get very close to an enemy, it might detect you. While stealthed, you move more slowly. In addition, many of the rogue's special attacks can only be executed while in stealth mode. Higher ranks of stealth improve the rogue's movement speed when sneaking.

The Druid

The druid is a formidable class with good healing ability, potent offensive spells, excellent buffs, and the unique ability to shapechange into different animal types. In its animal forms, the druid can adopt new roles, such as that of a warrior or rogue, giving it great versatility.

Allowable Races: Night Elf, Tauren

Primary Attributes: Intellect, Stamina, Spirit

Common Weapon Skills: Staves, Unarmed, One-Handed Maces or Daggers,

Advanced Weapon Skills: Daggers, Fist Weapons, Spears

Armor Proficiencies: Cloth, Leather

Class Abilities

Druid players have spells that cover three categories: healing, buffs, and offensive spells. They have healing spells that can heal immediately and over time. Their powerful buffs are among the best in the game, able to boost all attributes in addition to conferring strong armor and resistance bonuses. Their offensive spells, while good, are not meant as the druid's main strength.

SHAPESHIFTING

The druid's unique ability is shapeshifting, which allows the druid a choice of play styles. Once learned, these forms are activated just like casting a spell. While in an animal form, druids lose their spellcasting ability but gain a host of new abilities tailored to their new form.

In bear form, for example, druids are like warriors, gaining greater health, attack, and warrior abilities. In cat form, druids gain a tremendous boost to damage and stealth, and have access to rogue-like abilities. When in either bear or cat form, druids lose their mana bar and instead gain a rage or energy bar, respectively.

Druids can also learn non-combat forms that enable them to travel across land or water much more efficiently than most other classes.

As a druid levels up, it can learn new spells for its normal form, as well as additional abilities to enhance its animal forms.

SAMPLE DRUID SPELLS AND ABILITIES

This is a small sample of spells and abilities available to the druid. More fantastic spells and abilities are available at even higher levels.

 Entangling Roots: Temporarily roots the target in place, preventing it from moving. The roots also do slight damage over time. Higher-level root spells do more damage and root longer. This spell can only be cast outdoors.

 Faerie Fire: Decreases the armor of an enemy target. Also prevents the target from becoming invisible or using Stealth.

 Healing Touch: Quickly heals a target. Higher ranks add more health.

 Mark of the Wild: Boosts the target's armor. Higher ranks grant a higher armor bonus, magic resistance bonuses, and it boosts all of the target's attributes.

 Moonfire: Blasts the target for modest damage, and continues to deal damage over time. Higher ranks do more damage.

 Rejuvenation: Heals the target of a few hit points every few seconds. Although not adequate for immediate healing, higher ranks heal more over time.

 Starfire: Fires a bolt of damaging magic at the enemy. Higher ranks do more damage.

The Paladin

The paladin is a virtuous defender of the weak and a tireless enemy of the undead. Mixing elements of the warrior and the priest, the paladin is a tough melee fighter with great health, excellent protection, and very strong buffs. It also has a useful mix of healing and defensive spells. The tradition of holy knights is unique to the Alliance. In many ways, the paladin is the counterpart to the Horde's shaman, but geared towards physical battle more than spellcasting prowess.

Allowable Races: Dwarf, Human

Primary Attributes: Strength, Stamina, Intellect, Spirit

Common Weapon Skills: One-Handed Maces, Two-Handed Maces, Unarmed

Advanced Weapon Skills: Polearms, One-Handed Swords, Two-Handed Swords, One-Handed Axes, Two-Handed Axes

Armor Proficiencies: Cloth, Leather, Mail, Shield, Plate (Advanced)

Class Abilities

The paladin, like the warrior, can learn to wear all types of armor, and has among the widest selection of weapon skills. It has a good ability to thrive in melee combat, made even better with its unique buffs: auras and seals.

Auras are buffs that a paladin casts on itself that also have effect on all nearby party members. A paladin can only have one aura in effect at a time, and two paladins with the same aura cannot stack that aura's effects. However, multiple paladins can each use different auras to overlap different buffs on allies. Some auras can heal the paladin and his allies, boost armor, and damage attackers.

A seal is another kind of buff available to the paladin. Seals are short-term spell effects with specific benefits. Some seals increase damage dealt, absorb physical damage, or boost damage against undead. Only one seal at a time can be in effect on a player per paladin.

The remainder of the paladin's spells include healing, a resurrection spell, defensive spells, and spells specifically designed to attack undead.

SAMPLE PALADIN SPELLS AND ABILITIES

This is a small sample of spells and abilities available to the paladin. More fantastic spells and abilities are available at even higher levels.

 Devotion Aura: Boosts armor of all party members. Higher ranks add more armor.

 Divine Protection: Makes you immune to damage from physical combat and spells for a limited duration, but you cannot attack or cast spells during this time.

 Healing Aura: Heals party members over a short period of time. It is only active outside of combat. Higher ranks heal more.

 Holy Light: Heals one target of damage. Higher ranks heal more.

 Seal of Fury: Makes a friendly player more threatening, giving monsters greater desire to attack that player. A useful way for paladins to taunt monsters off weaker party members.

 Redemption: Brings a player back to life with full health and mana.

 Turn Undead: Forces an undead opponent to flee from the paladin for a few seconds.

The Shaman

Shamans are the spiritual advisors of the Horde. The shaman is a versatile and flexible class that fulfills many roles in an adventuring party. While other classes are pure fighters or spellcasters, the shaman enjoys a happy medium in between. The shaman is an effective spellcaster, but can also fight extremely well with mace and staff.

Allowable Races: Orc, Tauren, Troll

Primary Attributes: Intellect, Stamina, Spirit, Strength

Common Weapon Skills: One-Handed Maces, Staves, Unarmed

Advanced Weapon Skills: One-Handed Axes, Daggers, Fist Weapons

Armor Proficiencies: Cloth, Leather, Shield, Mail (Advanced)

Class Abilities

The shaman has good health and melee power, as well as spells designed to support the shaman in combat, such as instant-cast offensive spells and weapon buffs. It also has strong attack spells and heals.

The shaman's line-of-spirit spells enables it to perform a variety of useful non-combat actions. It can resurrect allies, turn into a ghost wolf for increased movement, or instantly teleport to a town.

Shaman Totems

The shaman's unique power is totems. Totems are spiritual objects that a shaman must earn through questing. Once earned, a totem enables a shaman to cast totem spells associated with that totem's element. Totem spells can be purchased from a trainer, although in order to cast a totem spell, the appropriate elemental totem must be carried in the shaman's inventory.

Casting a totem spell places a temporary ward on the ground that creates a spell effect in the area. This ward can be attacked by enemies, and the totem spell ends if the ward is destroyed. Totem spells can provide buffs, debuffs, healing, and they can attack enemies.

There are four totems. The first you can earn is earth, while the others are fire, water, and air. A shaman can have one totem from each element in effect at a time. Casting another totem spell from the same element as an existing totem causes the previous totem to disappear.

Earth totems tend to be protection spells, such as the stoneclaw totem that taunts monsters off the shaman, and the stoneskin totem, which reduces melee damage done by monsters. Fire totems, in contrast, tend to be offensive in nature, with spells such as searing totem, magma totem, and fire nova totem dealing damage to nearby enemies. Water and air totems offer several miscellaneous and useful spells. The mana spring totem (water), for instance, confers a large mana regeneration boost to the shaman and its allies, while the grounding totem (air) absorbs harmful spells cast by enemy spellcasters.

SAMPLE SHAMAN SPELLS AND ABILITIES

This is a small sample of spells and abilities available to the shaman. More fantastic spells and abilities are available at even higher levels.

 Astral Recall: Teleports the shaman back to its home base, which is selected by speaking to an innkeeper in any major town. This home base can be reset by speaking to a new innkeeper.

 Chain Lightning: Fires a bolt of lightning at an enemy, which then arcs to hit several other targets. Higher ranks do more damage.

 Earth Shock: Shocks the target, causing damage and disrupting any spell being cast by the target. This is an instant-cast spell. Higher ranks do more damage.

 Flametongue Weapon: Imbues the shaman's weapon with fire, giving it a chance to deal extra fire damage on each hit. A flametongue totem spell also exists that imbues the shaman's party members with this weapon property. Higher ranks do more fire damage.

 Frost Shock: Shocks the target for frost damage and slows the enemy's movement speed. This is an instant-cast spell. Higher ranks do more damage.

 Healing Wave: Heals a certain amount of damage. A healing totem spell also exists that heals the shaman's party members. Higher ranks heal more.

 Lightning Shield: Surrounds the shaman with balls of lightning that explode when the shaman is hit, causing damage to the attacker. Higher ranks do more damage.

The Hunter

The hunter is a unique class in World of Warcraft because it is primarily a ranged attacker. Even though other classes can learn to use ranged weapons, none of them is as proficient in their deadly use as the hunter. To support the hunter's ranged attacks, this class has two main advantages: a loyal pet and a wide array of movement-restricting spells.

Allowable Races: Dwarf, Night Elf, Tauren, Orc, Troll

Primary Attributes: Agility, Spirit, Intellect, Stamina

Common Weapon Skills: One-Handed Axes or Daggers, Guns or Bows, Unarmed

Advanced Weapon Skills: Crossbows, Fist weapons, Spears, Staves, One-Handed Swords, Two Handed Swords, Thrown, Two-Handed Axes

Armor Proficiencies: Cloth, Leather, Mail (Advanced)

Class Abilities

The hunter is a combat class, like the rogue and warrior, but whereas those classes rely on melee attacks, the hunter relies on ranged power. It does have spellcasting ability, but the hunter's spells are supportive ones, used to enhance the hunter's natural abilities.

To complement its ranged attacks, the hunter has a number of spells that imbue its gun or bow with additional damage, damage over time, or other magical effects.

Hunters also have a unique line-of-buff spells he can cast only on himself, which are called aspects. These spells emulate features of certain beasts. The aspect of the cheetah spell, for instance, boosts the hunter's movement speed, while the aspect of the monkey increases its dodge ability.

As a master of animals, the hunter also has a selection of beast control spells, in addition to spells that enhance his animal pet.

Hunter Pets

Pets are a key component of the hunter class. After the hunter gains some experience he can learn to tame the wild beasts of Azeroth. Using the beast taming spell, the hunter can select a beast in the wild and turn it into a loyal companion. The hunter's pet can then attack the hunter's target and keep it occupied while the hunter engages in ranged attacks.

A hunter's pet must be kept happy, or it will leave you or even turn on you. A hunter's pet has a happiness rating that you can see by clicking on your faithful beast's icon. As the pet fights, its happiness decreases, but happiness can be replenished by feeding your pet regularly.

Nearly any monster with the beast type can be tamed and turned into a pet. After you gain a new pet, you can train it in new abilities you acquire with the beast training ability.

If you find new pets you would like to tame, you can stable your current pet so that you have a selection of pets to choose from when you adventure in the world. You can only have one pet accompany you at a time. When a pet is not with you, it is kept in the stables, which can be found in most major cities.

SAMPLE HUNTER SPELLS AND ABILITIES

This is a small sample of spells and abilities available to the hunter. More fantastic spells and abilities are available at even higher levels.

 Auto Shot: Lets the hunter shoot its gun or bow automatically until this toggle is turned off. Only the hunter possesses the ability to auto shoot. All other classes must manually fire each shot.

 Aspect of the Pack: Makes the hunter and all party members move faster while this spell is active.

 Freezing Trap: Sets a trap that freezes the first enemy that approaches. This effect lasts a few seconds, but ends prematurely if the target is damaged. Only one trap can be active at a time. Lasts for one minute and can only be placed out of combat.

 Immolation Trap: Sets a trap on the ground that burns an enemy for damage over time. Only one trap can be active at a time. Lasts for one minute and can only be placed out of combat.

 Revive Pet: Restores your pet to life with minimal health.

 Serpent Sting: Adds a damage-over-time component to a hunter's ranged attack. Higher ranks do more damage.

 Wing Clip: A melee attack that does damage to the target and slows it down dramatically. Higher ranks do more damage.

The Warlock

Although many that consort with demons fall to darkness, the warlock class manages to bend demonic forces to its will without succumbing to pure evil. These spellcasters can summon demons to serve them, and they also cast many painful spells that slowly eat at the life of enemies. Warlocks are a physically weak class, but they compensate for this deficiency with their potent array of spells and their demonic pets.

Allowable Races: Gnome, Human, Orc, Undead

Primary Attributes: Intellect, Spirit, Stamina

Common Weapon Skills: Daggers, Unarmed, Wands

Advanced Weapon Skills: Staves, One-Handed Swords

Armor Proficiencies: Cloth

Class Abilities

Warlocks rely on their spells and their pets. The spells of a warlock fall into several general categories. Their curses can damage the target or weaken it physically. The warlock can also cast spells that damage the target over time. When several such spells are cast on a monster, they can rapidly deplete the target's health. The warlock also possesses some direct damage spells. Over time, the warlock can inflict as much damage as the mage with spells and pets, but it cannot defeat enemies as quickly. Although both classes are potent, the warlock's play style favors slow death for enemies, while the mage favors quick and explosive power.

Soul Shards

Many of the warlock's most powerful spells require the sacrifice of a reagent called a soul shard. Soul shards are obtained by killing a monster with the drain soul spell active. You only get a soul shard from a monster if you kill it or your party kills it, and then only if you receive experience for the kill.

Warlock Pets

Warlocks can acquire a pet at the start of play, and then acquire a different pet roughly as they gain experience and by completing a pet quest. Once acquired, a pet remains in the warlock's casting repertoire and can be summoned at will, although only one pet can be active at a time.

Warlock pets fulfill a variety of roles. The imp, for example, is a ranged attacker that can also cast protection spells on the warlock and party members. The voidwalker is a traditional melee combatant, with a great deal of health and a taunting ability. Higher-level pets have even more specialized roles, acting as high-damage rogues or even transportation.

Summoning a pet takes some time, and also expends a soul shard. The only pet that does not require a soul shard is the imp. The most powerful pets might even require two shards.

SAMPLE SPELLS AND ABILITIES

This is a small sample of spells and abilities available to the warlock. More fantastic spells and abilities are available at even higher levels.

 Create Soulstone: Creates a single-use soulstone that resurrects the owner. This can be given to other players. Requires the use of two soul shards. If you die while a soulstone is in your inventory, you can resurrect yourself using the stone, although you revive with minimal health and mana, and suffering resurrection sickness.

 Curse of Weakness: Reduces the damage that the afflicted target deals in melee combat. Higher ranks reduce damage further. Only one curse can be active on a target at a time.

 Drain Soul: Damages the target slowly over time. If the target dies while having its soul drained, the warlock automatically gains a soul shard. This is a channeled spell. Higher ranks do more damage, but still only provide one soul shard.

 Fear: Forces the target to flee in terror from the warlock for several seconds. During this time, the monster cannot attack, but it can call for help from allies. Higher ranks extend the duration of fear.

 Immolate: A fire spell that burns the target over time. Higher ranks do more damage.

 Life Tap: Converts some of the warlock's health into mana, damaging the warlock but replenishing mana by the same amount. This is an instant-cast spell. Higher ranks replenish more mana, but also do more damage to the caster.

 Ritual of Summoning: Summons another player from anywhere in the world to the warlock's location. Requires two helpers to cast the spell and consumes two soul shards. This spell is extremely useful for gathering party members together before embarking on quests.

Combat Pets

The two classes in World of Warcraft that have access to pets and rely heavily on them for success are the hunter and the warlock.

Pets are secondary characters that you can control. They are simpler and weaker than a full-fledged character class, but they provide extra power and support for your main character. Some pets are offensive in nature and join you in attacking your enemies. Some are more defensive, and occupy your target so you can attack from range without fear of retaliation. There are also more unusual pets with less easily defined abilities.

PET ABILITIES

Each pet has a small selection of abilities. No pet begins with more than a single ability or spell, but more can be learned through a pet trainer. The warlock pet trainer is called a demon trainer.

In order to train your pet in new abilities or spells, you must first summon the pet and then speak to a pet trainer. The pet's learnable spells and abilities then appear in the trainer's window. If you have no pet summoned, then the window will be blank.

Learning a new pet ability works like learning a class ability. Select the ability, and if your pet is of the appropriate level, click on the Train button to learn it. Pet abilities, like class spells, cost money to learn as well.

PET ACTION BAR

Your pet has an action bar that sits atop your own. This pet action bar only appears when you actually have a pet summoned. To attach your pet's spells and abilities to this bar, open the pet's spellbook or ability book, and drag the action to the bar just as you would for your own character. Actions on the bar can be used by clicking on the correct icon or pressing Ctrl and the corresponding hotkey number.

Chapter 7
Talents

Once a character achieves tenth level, it will begin earning talent points at the rate of one per level. Talent points can then be spent at the Talents window. Every class has three lines of talents, not including a character's racial talents list.

Talent points can be spent to purchase talents, which can do a variety of things. Many talents can improve your class' existing abilities, give you new abilities, or improve your class skills.

All classes have the same talent options, but no single character can hope to acquire every single talent. Thus, there are many talent choices open to your character, and your choices will help differentiate you from other players playing the same class.

Choosing Talents

Every class has three categories of talents that are organized by your class abilities. Mages, for instance, rely primarily on their spells, which are broken up into the arcane, frost, and fire schools. Thus, the mage's talent categories are arcane, frost, and fire. Each category can be accessed using the tabs at the bottom of the Talents window.

Talents are bought on a one-to-one ratio. One talent point spent on a talent gives you one rank in a talent. You do not accrue talent points until you have advanced past the first few levels of gameplay.

The talent system is tiered. There are low-level talents you must buy and master before you can learn high-level talents. However, you can see all talents in a category, and see the paths leading to all talents. In addition, mousing over any talent tells you what the talent does and what requirements you must meet to learn it.

Talents that are grayed out cannot be learned; either because you have no talent points to spend or because you do not have enough mastery of other talents. Talents do not have level limits.

Learning Talents

To learn a talent, mouse over the talent first and decide if it is right for you. Talents are difficult to unlearn, so you should be sure before you commit to one. Also keep in mind that you cannot learn every single talent, so you should make a choice about which talents or what category of talents you want to learn.

When you decide on a talent, left-click on it to learn it. There is no confirmation of your pick. Once you click on it, you buy it. If by purchasing the talent you open new avenues of talents, the newly unlocked talents will turn from gray to bright.

All classes have talents that allow the player to customize their character. Talents can be applied in the following ways:

♦   To improve a class' existing spells or abilities.

♦   To alter the functionality of existing class spells or abilities.

♦   To acquire new spells and abilities.

♦   To improve class skills.

The three lines of class talents are geared towards each class' main strengths. For example, mages naturally divide their talents into arcane, frost, and fire, which mimic the three main schools of magic mages learn. Warriors have the talent lines of arms, fury, and protection. Each category of talents is designed like a tree, with new talents branching out from a core set of base talents you can learn at low levels. Within each tree, a character can learn talents that make that character more effective in all the abilities and capabilities that fall under the heading of that talent tree. The frost line of talents, for example, enhances a mage's proficiency with frost spells. The warrior's protection talents improve the warrior's taunt and defensive abilities.

No player can ever hope to become a master of all three lines of talents. In fact, with dozens of talents per line, and multiple ranks to each talent, the most a character could hope to fully master is one talent tree, and perhaps half of another one.

Talents can be seen by clicking on the Talents button or pressing the hotkey N. Mouse over each talent to receive a description of what it is and how to use it. Be sure to peruse your class' entire array of talents before choosing them. It helps to have a goal or general theme for your character when purchasing talents, rather than picking them haphazardly. Of course, there is nothing wrong with experimentation, but you may find it wise to research all your class' talents before purchasing them.

Chapter 8
Skills

Skills are an important aspect of your character. Class skills establish how effective you are in your class abilities; weapon and armor skills determine what offensive and defensive equipment you can use; and trade skills let you gather raw materials and turn them into finished goods you can use or sell.

CLASS SKILLS

You can see all your skills, including class skills, by opening up your Skills page by hitting the hotkey K or flipping to it from your Character Info window.

Class skills are at the top of the Skills page and are specific to a character class. When a mage, for example, casts fire or frost spells, the mage uses the fire or frost skill to determine how effective these spells are. The higher the mage's rating in these class skills, the harder the mage's spells are to resist.

Non-spellcasters also have class skills attached to their abilities, and these skills likewise dictate how effective those abilities are when used.

Improving Class Skills

Class skills improve when you use them. When you cast a spell or use an ability, the associated skill sometimes improves by one point. Note that trade skills, weapons skills, and defense skills do not increase automatically as you gain levels.

Maximum Class Skill Level

The maximum score you can have in a class skill is determined by your level, and if your class skills are already at their maximum, you will not gain any more class-related skill points, no matter how many more times you cast spells or use class abilities. However, when you level up, the cap for your class skills increases, and you can again earn more class-related skill points.

Weapon Skills and
Armor Proficiencies

All classes also have a defined set of weapon skills and armor proficiencies. Warriors, for example, can learn to use all armor and weapon types (with the exception of wands), while mages can only use cloth armor and daggers, staves, wands, or swords.

In addition there are race restrictions on weapon skills. Gnome warriors, for example, cannot use bows, while Night Elf warriors can't use guns.

A high score in a weapon skill improves your chance to hit when using that kind of weapon. In contrast, armor proficiency does not improve with use; once you have an armor proficiency, you can wear any armor of that type.

Improving Weapon Skills

Your weapon skills only improve if you use them. Thus, if your character has the dagger skill, but always uses staves and not daggers your staff skill increases, while your dagger skill never improves.

With all weapon skills, the higher the rating, the better you are at using that skill. Therefore, if you switch from staves to daggers at high level, your dagger skill will start out too low to penetrate the defense of monsters of your same level.

Learning New Armor and Weapon Skills

New weapon skills and armor proficiencies can be learned by visiting a class trainer. In your training window will be listed any weapon skills or armor proficiencies available to your class, as well as the minimum level you must be in order to learn them.

If the skill or proficiency is unattainable for your level, it will be in red text. If it is learnable, it will be in green text. Learning a new weapon skill or armor proficiency only costs money. As long as you have enough money, you can simply click on the Learn button at the bottom of the training window and your character will be automatically updated with the new weapon skill or armor proficiency.

TRADE SKILLS

Trade skills enable players to harvest resources from the environment and then turn these resources into finished products that players can use or sell. Any player can learn any trade skill, regardless of class.

Learning Trade Skills

Players do not start with knowledge of any trade skills. To learn a trade skill, you must find a trade skill trainer and then learn the skill from the trainer by paying skill points.

After you learn a trade skill, the skill is added to your Abilities book. To find it, open your Abilities book and turn to the Abilities page. You can use the skill by left-clicking on it from this page. Alternatively, you can click and drag the ability to your action bar and use it from there.

The Two Trade Skill Limit

Every character can learn up to two trade skills. This enables a player to be self-sufficient and choose one gathering trade skill and one production trade skill. Alternatively, you could learn two gathering trade skills or two production trade skills. No character can learn more than two trade skills. However, secondary skills, such as fishing and cooking, do not fall under this restriction.

Trade Skill Ranks

When you first learn a trade skill, you gain apprentice status in that skill. As you use the trade skill, either by gathering materials or making items, you will improve your skill. Once you hit a skill level of 75, you will then have to earn the next rank of craftsmanship in your trade skill, which is journeyman rank. When you raise your skill level another 75 points to 150, you will need to then learn the next rank, expert, and so on.

Finding initial skill trainers in the game is easy, as they are located in any number of settlements, but to learn the most advanced trade skill techniques, you will have to journey far and wide to seek out the masters of your trade skill. In some cases, expert ranks and beyond will only be taught to players that complete a quest for the trade skill trainer.

Unlearning Trade Skills

You can unlearn trade skills by opening up your Skills window (hotkey K or click on the Skills tab from the Character Info panel). Then click on the trade skill. At the bottom of the Skills window is crossed out circle next to the selected trade skill. Click on that to unlearn the skill. Unlearning a trade skill frees up a slot for you to learn a new trade skill, but it also erases all skill points you have accumulated in that skill. If you later relearn the trade skill, you will not resume it at your last skill level, but must start from the bottom again.

GATHERING TRADE SKILLS

Gathering trade skills let you harvest raw materials from the environment. Throughout the game world, there are mineral nodes, plants, and animal corpses. These objects can be harvested to gather ore and stones, herbs, and skins.

Using a Gathering Trade Skill

Any time you mouse over a resource, a gathering icon appears by your cursor. Mousing over a mineral node brings up a pickaxe cursor; mousing over a plant brings up a flower cursor; and mousing over a skinnable corpse brings up a skinning knife cursor.

The tool tip that appears when you mouse over the resource tells you the name of the resource and the name of the skill necessary for harvesting it. The skill name appears in a different color, depending on how difficult the resource is to harvest. If you do not have the skill at all, then the color of the skill name is red, meaning you can't harvest it. The name is also red if you have the skill, but the resource is beyond your skill level to gather. In that case, you must improve your skill level before you can successfully harvest the resource.

Improving Your Gathering Trade Skill

As with all trade skills, you can improve your trade skill by using it. Every time you harvest a resource using your gathering skill, you have a chance of increasing your skill by one.

The color, and therefore difficulty, of the skill name in the tool tip tells you how likely you are to improve your skill when you harvest it. The more difficult the resource is to harvest, the more likely you are to gain a skill point when you do so. The levels of difficulty, from least to most, are as follows: gray, green, yellow, orange, and red. If you harvest a yellow or orange resource, you will usually gain a skill increase. If you harvest a green resource, you will rarely get a skill increase, and if you harvest a gray resource, you will never get a skill increase. Red resources, of course, cannot be harvested at your current skill level.

As you improve your gathering skill level, you will eventually be able to harvest more difficult resources.

Buying Ingredients

Many production trade skills require certain trade supplies in addition to the other blueprint ingredients. For the tailoring trade skill, you always need thread to sew together the cloth pieces, while many blacksmithing recipes require flux to remove the impurities of the metals.

These trade supplies can be purchased from a trade supply vendor, who can often be found in any major city or town.

Ingredients for High Level Items

Once you begin making higher-level items, the ingredients you need become more varied. High level tailoring items require leather, while high level mining and engineering items often require both leather and linen. Many high level ingredients cannot be bought from vendors, and instead must be purchased from other players or found as loot from monsters.

Herbalism

Herbalism lets you gather herbs from the many plants around the world. Low-level herbs include peacebloom flowers, silverleaf, and snakeroot. Higher-level herbs include mageroyal, briarthorn, bruiseweed, kingroyal, and goldthorn.

Herbalism Tips: To harvest an herb, simply right-click on it. If you have the necessary skill level, you'll almost always open a loot window containing the herbs you've found. If you get a message telling you that you failed to harvest the herb, simply retry it.

When you first learn the herbalism skill, you acquire the find herb ability. Clicking on it makes all nearby herbs appear on your minimap. Bright dots on the minimap are herbs above ground, while grayed out dots are herbs in caves below ground. You can activate the find herbs ability, and it will remain active until you die, or until you turn it off.

The herbs you gain from this skill are used to make potions with alchemy or to enchant items with the enchanting skill. If you choose the herbalism gathering skill, choosing either alchemy or enchanting is a logical next choice to improve your character. You can also sell the herbs you find to other players.

Mining

Mining lets you gather ore, stone, and gems. Ore can be turned into metal bars, while stones can be turned into refined stones. Metal bars are especially important in all blacksmithing and engineering blueprints. Gems are required for many high-level blueprints in other production skills. At low levels, you can mine copper, but as you improve your skill, you can learn to mine tin, silver, iron, gold, and mithril.

Mining Tips: In order to mine a mineral node, you must have a mining pick in your backpack or inventory bags. You can then right-click on a node to gather minerals from it. In order to smelt raw ore into metal bars, you need a forge. Forges are located in all major cities.

When you first learn the mining skill, you gain the find minerals ability. Clicking on it makes all nearby mineral nodes appear on your minimap. Minerals that are above ground appear as bright dots on the map, while minerals below ground appear as gray dots. You can activate the find minerals ability, and it will remain active until you die, or until you turn it off.

The minerals you harvest are needed most in blacksmithing and engineering. If you choose the mining skill, the next logical choice is one of those two production skills. You can also sell your minerals, as they are always in demand.

Skinning

Skinning lets you gather leather and hides from fallen monsters. Only beasts are skinnable. Humanoids, demons, undead, and other monster types do not leave behind skinnable corpses. Your skinning level determines what level of corpse you can skin. A player with apprentice skinning will not be able to skin a level-40 corpse, for instance. Low-level corpses provide ruined leather scraps and light leather, while higher-level corpses provide medium, heavy, and thick leather. You can also find light, medium, and heavy hides.

Skinning Tips: You must have a skinning knife in your inventory in order to skin a corpse. To do so, simply right-click on the corpse.

Leather is used primarily in the leatherworking production skill, but is also required in several tailoring, blacksmithing, and engineering blueprints.

Once you choose skinning, it is a logical next step to choose leatherworking as a production skill. You can also sell the leather you gather, as it is always in demand.

PRODUCTION TRADE SKILLS

Production trade skills enable you to make items that can be worn by players and sold in the World of Warcraft economy. Production skills are an excellent way to equip your character with armor and weapons you can't find anywhere else in the game, and a great way to make money as well.

Using Production Skills

Using a production skill requires a blueprint of an item, and the ingredients specified in that blueprint. When you have gathered all the ingredients in your inventory, open your production trade skill window from the Abilities book or from the trade skill icon on your action bar. A list of all the blueprints you have appears in the trade skill window.

The item window at the bottom of the trade skill window shows you how many of each ingredient you have, while the blueprint list tells you how many copies you can make.

When you are ready, click "Create", and after a brief amount of time, the necessary ingredients will be taken from your bag. Then the newly produced item will appear in your inventory.

Making an item with a production skill is always a success. As long as you have all the required ingredients, your item will be made without failure.

Improving Your Production Trade Skill

Production skills improve as you use them. You increase your skill when you make difficult items, but not when you make easy ones. All production blueprints are color-coded for difficulty. From easiest to hardest, these colors are as follows: gray, green, yellow, orange, and red. Red skills never show up in your blueprint list because you cannot learn them, but you can browse them when seeing the trade skill trainer. Creating orange items always increase your skill; yellow items sometimes increase your skill; green items rarely increase your skill; and gray items never increase your skill.

As you improve your trade skill, blueprints that were orange can turn yellow, green, and eventually gray. To improve your skill further, you must find more challenging blueprints to add to your list.

Finding Ingredients

Production skills require massive amounts of raw materials to use. These materials are sometimes called ingredients or components. Many can be acquired by gathering the necessary resources using the associated gathering skill. You can also acquire the necessary ingredients by buying them from other players. When making higher-level skill items, you'll have to get different ingredients anyway, as these blueprints often require a wide range of components.

Acquiring Blueprints

The blueprints to make an item are called different things depending on what trade skill they fall under: plans, schematics, formulae, recipes, patterns, and more.. When you first learn a production trade skill, you are provided with a few blueprints. Most other blueprints are bought from an appropriate trade skill vendor. Blueprints you buy from vendors have a minimum skill level before you can purchase them.

While many blueprints only come from vendors, some blueprints can also be found as rare loot from monsters, as quest rewards, or purchased from other players. All blueprints, except for the ones you get when you first learn a skill, have a required skill level before you can use them. Blueprints found as loot from monsters must be scribed manually into your trade skill blueprint list by right-clicking on them from your inventory.

Once acquired, the blueprint is added to your blueprint list for the trade skill.

Alchemy

Alchemy enables you to brew potions, oils, and other substances. Potions are imbibed by players and provide various benefits, while oils are applied to weapons and armor for added effect.

Blueprints are called: Recipes

Blacksmithing

Blacksmithing lets you make weapons and metal armors. It is an extremely useful skill and can earn you significant cash, since you can make weapons usable by all classes. In order to turn metal bars and other ingredients into finished arms and armor, you must work at an anvil, which can be found in all major cities. Many of the ingredients necessary for blacksmithing can be gathered with the mining skill, so that it is a useful secondary skill for prospective smiths.

Blueprints are called: Plans

Engineering

Engineering is a production skill that lets you create a bizarre mix of clockwork contraptions, explosives, goggles, and guns. Among the production trade skills, this one requires some of the widest ranges of materials. However, most blueprints require at least some metal or stone, so prospective engineers should also pick up the mining skill.

Blueprints are called: Schematics

Leatherworking

Leatherworking lets you create leather armor, leather patches that can boost defense, and containers. All leatherworking blueprints require leather and cured hides, so prospective leatherworkers should also pick up the skinning skill.

Blueprints are called: Patterns

Tailoring

Tailoring enables you to create cloth armor. Tailoring and leather-working are the only skills that let you create bags, which are used to hold additional items in their inventory. Thus, tailors are often in high demand. Tailoring blueprints require various types of cloth. The most common type of cloth is linen, followed by wool, silk, and mageweave. The best tailoring items can only be made out of the rarest cloths, such as silk and mageweave. Cloth cannot be collected with a gathering skill, but instead must be looted from fallen humanoid monsters, which sometimes drop cloth as loot.

Blueprints are called: Patterns

First Aid

The first aid skill lets you create bandages that you can apply on yourself and on other players to cure hit point damage. First aid also lets you make other curative aids, such as anti-venom. Applying a first aid bandage requires a brief amount of time, but it is a great way to replenish health if you aren't adventuring with a healer. The first aid skill is also a great complementary skill for warriors and rogues who like to play solo. In order to make bandages, you need cloth. The best bandages require the rarest cloths, such as silk and mageweave.

First Aid Tips: You can trade bandages to other players, but they cannot use them unless they also have the first aid skill. You can also apply first aid bandages to other players. If you receive a bandage, you cannot be bandaged again for a minute. Unlike potions, bandages take a brief time to use, so they are more suited for use after or before battle.

Blueprints are called: Formulas

Enchanting

The enchanting skill lets you place various magic abilities on equipment. You can enchant equipment to have attribute bonuses, damage enhancements, spell protection, and even skill boosts. The enchanting skill does not require a gathering skill, since the main ingredients for this trade skill are actual magic items. Enchanters can disenchant magic items (those that are green or blue in color), and turn them into the basic enchanting ingredients that are then used to create successful enchantments. Aside from these basic ingredients, some recipes also call for the occasional herb or odd object. All enchanting recipes also require that you have a rod in your inventory before you can cast them.

Enchanting Tips: Since you do not create a tradable item with enchanting, you must enchant other people's equipment through the trade window. At the bottom of each player's trade window is a single non-tradable slot. Once another player places an item in this slot, you can click on it to enchant it. The enchantment will not be complete until both players then click the trade button at the bottom of the window.

Blueprints are called: Formulas

Secondary Skills

Secondary skills are useful skills that you can learn these without using up your two trade skill slots. However, you learn them and improve them just as you would trade skills.

Fishing

Fishing is a special type of gathering trade skill that does not work like the others. There are no fishing nodes in the game. Instead, when you want to gather fish, you simply take your fishing pole and use it at a body of water. A fishing bobber appears at the end of your line, and when it moves, you click it to reel in your catch.

Unlike the other gathering trade skills, you cannot click on a body of water to see if it is fishable or not. Nor can you see how challenging the body of water is and therefore how likely you are to skill up by fishing there. However, bodies of water in low-level zones are easier to fish than those in high-level zones.

Cooking

The cooking skill is used mainly to make food out of raw meat. Food can then be eaten by players to replenish health. This production skill does not require an associated gathering skill, since all fallen beasts drop meat, but the fishing skill provides plenty of raw meat to turn into food. Once you gather the necessary ingredients for a cooking recipe, you need to have a cooking pot or cooking fire nearby in order to make the food. These can be found in most major cities and towns.

Chapter 9
The World

The world of Azeroth is an epic land of adventure, filled with towering settlements, exotic locales, hidden riches, and friendly allies.

MOVING THROUGH THE WORLD

Navigating the vast twin landmasses of Kalimdor and the Eastern Kingdoms can be daunting, but there are many ways to explore the world of Warcraft.

Note

Throughout this manual and in the game itself, you will find the name Azeroth used in two different contexts. Azeroth is both the name of the world of Warcraft, and the name of one of the three continents that comprise the Eastern Kingdoms, the landmass opposite of Kalimdor on the world map. The other two continents of the Eastern Kingdoms are Loch Modan in the center and Lordaeron in the north. Sometimes you will see reference to Azeroth the world, and other times you will see reference to Azeroth the continent.

Zones

Both Kalimdor and the Eastern Kingdoms are split into regions called zones. Within each zone are many locales. When you enter a new locale or zone, its name will appear briefly at the top of your screen, telling you that you have entered a new area. Your zone is important to note because many elements of the game are organized by zone. For example, the quests in your quest log are organized by zone, and certain messages in your chat log are restricted to your current zone.

Moving between zones is seamless, with no waiting or loading time. The exception is when you cross into an instanced dungeon or a new continent.

Beginner Zones

When you first enter the game with a level-one character, you appear in a low-level zone for beginners. This region is sometimes called a newbie zone by more experienced players in the game. The monsters here are generally easy to defeat, and there are several quests to help you get started in exploring the world, battling enemies, and earning some treasure. For levels one to five, you'll usually stay inside your beginning area, and you won't have to wander into new ones.

By the time you exceed level five, you will begin to find new quests that send you to more challenging areas of the world. In fact, World of Warcraft is a game that is constantly shepherding you to new venues of the world to explore. As a general rule of thumb, expect to be exposed to an entirely new zone every ten levels or so.

For the first few levels, everything you need is so close that you can easily reach every place you need to go in a matter of minutes. However, once you've discovered more than one zone, you will find new modes of transportation to take you across the vast distances between the many locales you uncover.

Intercity Travel: Aerial Mounts

Each zone usually has a major city or town that acts as the capital or main trading post of the zone. Many of these settlements have a local flight master, an NPC who can ferry you between cities on a flying beast for a nominal fee. The type of beast you can ride varies according to your faction, but all of them do the same thing. They provide rapid transportation between cities, allowing you to fly across the continent. In many cases, a journey that might take half an hour on foot would take just minutes by air.

IDENTIFYING FLIGHT MASTERS

You can tell flight masters apart from other non-player characters by the winged boot icon that appears when you mouse over them. In addition, flight masters have a green exclamation point over their heads if you have not yet discovered the flight destination they represent.

USING FLYING MOUNTS

In order to use the flying mount transportation system, you have to find and right-click the flight master. A small flight path map appears on your screen showing you all the flight paths you have acquired, provided you have at least two connected flight path destinations. To fly to one of the destinations on the opened map, simply left-click on it to begin the flight.

ADDING FLIGHT PATHS

Flight is only allowed between cities for which you have a flight path. To find a flight path to a city, you must first get there by foot or some other means, and greet the local flight master. There is only one flight master in a settlement, and not all settlements have one.

When you click on a particular flight master for the first time, a message appears on screen telling you that you have discovered the flight path to the city. The flight path will now be added to the flight path map any time you click on a flight master on the same continent, thus allowing travel to the city from then on. Flying mount transportation is only available within a continent.

CROSS-FACTION USE

This mode of travel is also faction specific: Horde players can't use Alliance flying mounts, and Alliance players cannot use Horde aerial mounts. There are no flight paths across the ocean linking Kalimdor and Azeroth. However, there are other ways to cross the Great Sea between the continents.

Cross-Continental Travel

Crossing the violent Great Sea that separates the continents is a journey that can only be made by sturdy ship or airborne zeppelin. Each faction – Horde and Alliance – has at least one means of inter-continental travel between Kalimdor and the Eastern Kingdoms.

ALLIANCE TRAVEL

Alliance players use ships to traverse the Great Sea. The Alliance ship routes link Auberdine and Theramore in Kalimdor to Menethil in the Eastern Kingdoms.

HORDE TRAVEL

Horde players can travel between the continents by using goblin-operated zeppelins. These zeppelins connect the cities of Orgrimmar in Kalimdor and Grom'Gol in Azeroth with the Undercity in Lordaeron.

NEUTRAL TRAVEL

Both Horde and Alliance players also have a second method of intercontinental travel common to both of them, and that is the goblin shipping company. This neutral ship operation connects Booty Bay in Azeroth and Ratchet in Kalimdor, and can be used by all players.

BOARDING YOUR VESSEL

As with aerial mount travel, only Horde players may use the Horde zeppelins, and only Alliance players may use the Alliance ships. However, unlike with flight masters, the travel destinations by ship or zeppelin are already unlocked for you. All you need to do is go to a dock if you are boarding a ship or a zeppelin tower if you are embarking a zeppelin. When your vessel pulls in, just hop aboard. If your vessel isn't there, simply wait a few minutes. Vessels arrive regularly and the wait between them is only a few minutes.

LENGTH OF JOURNEY
The roundtrip between two destinations usually only takes five minutes, with a pause of roughly one minute at each dock to wait for passengers.

WHILE IN TRANSIT
While you are riding on either a zeppelin or ship, you are free to move within the confines of your vessel. You can also jump overboard, however this is not advisable. If you jump overboard while aboard a zeppelin you will most likely fall to your death. You also might not be able to reach your corpse to revive yourself. The fall off a ship isn't as lethal, but you could die of fatigue while treading water waiting for the next ship. It's advisable to stay inside your ship or zeppelin until you arrive at your destination.

Hearthstones and Home

In World of Warcraft, your character can choose an inn to use as his or her home. Inns exist in most major cities, and are a place of rest. If you leave your character in an inn and log out of the game from there, your character will accumulate a rest bonus (see Chapter 5: Your Character for more details).

To declare an inn as your home base, you must first find the inn you wish to rest at and talk to the innkeeper. Tell the innkeeper that you want to make the current inn your home, according to the pop-up window.

The innkeeper then gives you a hearthstone bound to that inn. The hearthstone takes up one slot in your inventory bag. Any time you want to be transported to your home inn, right-click on your hearthstone. After a short casting time, you will be teleported back to your home inn. A hearthstone can only be used every 60 minutes, so after you use a hearthstone, you must wait another hour before you can use it again.

You can only have one home base at a time, but you can always change your home by speaking to a new innkeeper in a new town.

A hearthstone is a great way to exit a dungeon or move across continents without going through aerial mounts, boats, or zeppelins. It is also useful to ensure that you always log out of the game in an inn for the largest rest bonus possible.

Other Modes of Travel

MOUNTS

Once you achieve a very high level, you can purchase a mount to serve as your primary mode of transportation within a continent. Mounts travel much faster than normal characters, but they are very expensive. Only the wealthiest of high-level characters have the means to buy mounts. Each race has its own unique type of mount, except for tauren, who are too big to ride animals and must resort to their plainsrunning racial ability. Warlocks and paladins of any race do not need to buy mounts since they can earn class-specific mounts through quests.

TRAVEL FORMS

Druids and shaman can learn spells that transform them into animals for increased movement speed. While in these travel forms, they can move much faster than normal players.

SPELLS

The mage, shaman, and warlock all have spells useful for instantaneous transportation across the world.

SETTLEMENTS

The world of Warcraft is a vibrant place full of wild dangers, but also great civilization. The shining centers of safety and culture in Azeroth are settlements.

There are settlements of varying sizes dispersed around the world of Warcraft. The largest such settlements are the racial capital cities. These are the human city of Stormwind, the dwarven city of Ironforge, the night elf city of Darnassus, the orc city of Orgrimmar, the undead city of Undercity, and the tauren city of Thunder Bluff. Gnomes share the dwarven city and trolls share the orc city. In these cities you can find most class trainers, trade skill trainers, flight masters, most merchants, inns, and banks. The leaders of each race also make these capitals their home, and many quests will originate and end there.

Other smaller settlements are located in various zones throughout the world. In general, most beginning and intermediate zones have at least one main settlement and several smaller settlements.

Most major settlements that aren't the size of capitals, including the goblin ports of Booty Bay and Ratchet, will have inns and merchants. Some of them might have class or trade skill trainers. Most of these settlements, though, at least have an inn. However the outposts in the most remote zones might not even have that

Settlement Amenities

These are some of the amenities you can find in a settlement. Only the greatest of cities will have them all, but most have at least an inn and a few merchants.

INNS

Inns are situated in most cities and camps, and provide players a place to rest. If you log out in an inn, your character will accumulate rest bonus faster so that the next time you login to play, you'll earn more experience for kills. Inns also have merchants that will sell you food.

BANKS

Only large cities have banks, where players can store items they do not wish to carry. Banks across Azeroth are linked so you can access your storage from any bank in the world by talking to a banker NPC.

MERCHANTS

Larger settlements will have the most merchants, including specific ones devoted entirely to trade skill ingredients, armor types, and more specialized items. Smaller settlements might only have a general goods merchant for the most common items. To find the widest range of items, you will need to venture to large cities and capitals, but if you need only simple items like food or drink, you can usually find those at any town.

TRAINERS

The class trainers for all the classes usually can only be found in capitals and major cities. Even then, capital cities usually will only have trainers for classes specific to their main population. You won't find paladin trainers in the tauren city of Thunder Bluff, for example. Trade skill trainers, on the other hand, are more common, although you still won't find them in remote towns or camps.

FLIGHT MASTERS

Most zones have at least one major settlement with a flight master to connect the zone to other flight paths in the continent.

There is no hard rule about what each settlement has. You have to explore them yourself, or ask in the general chat channel, to find out what non-player characters reside in each settlement.

Non-Player Characters

A non-player character is technically any character in the game that is not controlled by a human player. However, most players use the term NPC to refer to a friendly humanoid, and refer to creatures as enemies or monsters. Some examples of NPCs are quest givers, bankers, auctioneers, merchants, flight masters trainers, and guards.

You can tell friendly NPCs apart from other characters because they have green names. In addition, the tool tip text for an NPC will indicate what kind of NPC it is, such as a trainer or merchant NPCs of the opposite faction, while friendly to opposing players are hostile to you, and so they appear with red names.

Despite the presence of so many NPCs, you can only interact with some of them. Many guards and citizens are not interactive. You can tell if an NPC is open to interaction if the cursor changes shape when you mouse over the character. Most interactive NPCs stay in one place. That means they do not wander, so it is easier to find them However, some quest giving NPCs occasionally patrol a small path

Interaction Icons

If you can talk to an NPC, the mouse cursor changes from a hand to a chat balloon when you mouse over that NPC. NPCs that offer the chat icon usually give you quests, gossip, or information when you right-click on them.

If the NPC is a merchant, then the mouse cursor changes to a purse. Right-clicking on the merchant opens up a trading window, and allows you to buy and sell items.

If the NPC is a class or trade skill trainer, then your cursor will turn into a book when you mouse over the individual. Right-clicking on the trainer opens the training window and lets you learn new abilities or spells.

Some NPCs have multiple roles, such as being both vendors and quest givers. When you mouse over these NPCs, your cursor will offer the chat balloon only. Once you click on the NPC to talk to it, you get a dialog box that then allows you to choose how you want to interact with it.

When you mouse over certain characters, your cursor might also change into a sword. If this happens, then that NPC is a hostile enemy and you can attack it. Only characters that change your cursor to a sword, including all monsters, can be attacked. All other non-player characters are immune to attacks.

Economy

Merchants

The merchants, or vendors, in World of Warcraft are important non-player characters. They are your default means of buying and selling equipment, as well as the supplier of many materials necessary for making items with your trade skills. Food and drink, which keep your health and mana replenished, are also easily bought from merchants throughout the game world.

Buying and Selling

When you wish to buy an item from a merchant, right-click on him or her. The merchant's inventory window will pop up, showing you the items for sale. In some cases, the merchant will have more than one window of items. Each item in the merchant's inventory contains a small picture and the name of the item. If you mouse over the item, you will see more information about it. The item's price is displayed under its name and to the right of its icon. Items that the merchant has in limited quantity have a number in the top left corner of the item's picture, displaying how many of that item the merchant has in stock.

To buy an item, simply right-click on it, or click and drag it into one of your bag slots. You will not be prompted to confirm your purchase, so be sure you want the item before you right-click on it.

Selling an item is easier than buying one, since you can go to any merchant to sell. If you wish to sell an item from your inventory, right-click on any merchant. Mousing over an item in your inventory shows you the price you will get if you sell it. Some items have no selling price. To sell an item, right-click on it or drag it to the merchant window. You will not be prompted to confirm your sale, so be sure you want to sell the item before you click on it.

Types of Merchants

There are different kinds of merchants in the game, and each type sells a different set of wares. It is important to know at a glance what each merchant sells so you can more efficiently stock up on your needed provisions and equipment. Not all these merchants will be available in each settlement. Only the largest capitals have all the vendors available within their city limits.

MERCHANTS CAN BE GROUPED
INTO THE FOLLOWING CATEGORIES

Goods: General goods merchants sell a hodgepodge of goods such as food, drink, bags, and ammunition, consolidating some of the most common items from several different merchants into one vendor. Trade suppliers do the same thing, but sell basic trade skill materials instead.

Food and Drink Vendors: These merchants, who include bakers, butchers, mushroom sellers, and grocers, sell food that replenishes health and drinks that restore mana.

Trade Skill Vendors: These merchants sell the materials necessary for using your trade skill. They include tailoring good vendors, leatherworkers, blacksmiths, and fishing vendors.

Armor Merchants: Leatherworkers sell leather armor; clothiers sell cloth armor; and armorers sell mail and plate armor.

Weapons Merchants: Weaponsmiths sell a variety of weapons while bowyers and gunsmiths sell ammo and ranged weapons.

There are also unique merchants throughout the world, many of them goblins, who have a rotating stock of powerful magic items and trade skill blueprints. They often roam the wilderness between towns in higher-level zones.

From time to time, trade skill merchants will also sometimes have special items for sale that rotate in and out of stock. Check back with merchants to see if they have any new blueprints for sale.

Player Economy

When buying or selling items from merchants, you cannot bargain. Their prices are set. However, you can often get better value by buying or selling from other player characters.

The player economy in World of Warcraft is a robust one. There are two ways to buy or sell items to the player community: advertising them in the trade channel or using auction houses.

Trade Channel

To sell or buy an item over the trade channel, open up your chat prompt and type /trade, followed by your message. Doing this ensures that your message is displayed in the trade channel and not in general chat. Most trade requests in the general channel are ignored by players and you cannot link items in General Chat.

If you have an item for sale, your message should include the item you want to sell, the quantity of items, and your asking price. If you wish to have the players in the trade channel bid on your item, you should say so. All bidding should then be done in the trade channel, and not through private messaging.

If you are selling your item for a flat rate, state that as well. You can have any prospective buyer respond in the trade channel or send you a private message.

If you wish to buy an item in the trade channel, state your needs, the quantity you want, and the price you are willing to pay.

The trading that goes on in the trade channel in World of Warcraft is restricted to your current city only. Sometimes, if you are not finding a good market for your items, you might want to go to a new city and try advertising your trade again. In World of Warcraft, the player-run economy is a free-market one where prices can fluctuate greatly depending on the time of day and the zone in question. It can be very exciting to trade with other players, although certain etiquette should be observed in order to ensure fair and respectful conduct. Only bid on items you are serious about purchasing, and try to coordinate an exchange of money and goods as quickly as possible once the auction is concluded.

Linking Items for Sale

If you are buying or selling an item, you should link the item to your chat message so that prospective buyers can see the item for sale. To do that, open your chat prompt, type your message, and then link the item by holding down the shift key and clicking on the item from your bag slot. The item will appear in brackets and color coded for the item's rarity. Other players that see the linked item in chat can click on it to open up the item's info box.

Auction Houses

Another way to buy and sell items is through auctioneers at the auction houses. There are three auction houses in the world: a Horde auction house in Orgrimmar, an Alliance auction house in Ironforge, and a neutral auction house in the goblin city of Gadgetzan. Auctioneers exist within these auction houses and allow you to buy or sell items without having to go through the trade channel.

If you have an item to sell, you can drop it off at the auctioneer, set a bid price and length of auction, and let the auctioneer handle the rest. When the item sells, you get your money in the mail. If you wish to buy an item from an auctioneer, you can browse the items up for auction and make a bid. If you win the bid, the item is then mailed to you through the in-game mail system.

Browsing Items for Auction

To see what items are up for auction in a city, speak to any of the auctioneers in the auction house to open the auction window. The initial window is blank, except for fields and filters that you can use to refine your item search.

FILTER LIST

On the left are filters that let you search for weapons, armor, containers, consumables, trade goods, projectiles, quivers and ammo pouches, trade skill blueprints, reagents, and miscellaneous items. Trade Goods include most gathering skill resources, such as herbs and ore. After you click on a filter, click on the Search button to list all the relevant items up for auction in the city.

ADVANCED SEARCHING

You can refine your search further by specifying the name, level range, and quality of the item you are looking for. You can also restrict the search to only items that you can use by clicking on the Usable Items check-box.

SEARCHING FOR A SPECIFIC ITEM

To search for a specific item, type its name in the name field and click the Search button.

SEARCH RESULTS

All items that meet the criteria of your search appear in the main auction window. Each entry includes a picture of the item, its name, level requirement, the duration of the auction, the high bidder, and the current bid price, or minimum required bid if the item has no current bidder. If the seller has left an option to buy the item outright, then the buyout price will be listed after the current bid price in parentheses.

To see more information on the selected item, mouse over the item picture to open its info box. Items you cannot use are displayed in red.

Placing a Bid

If you see an item you wish to bid on, click on it. At the bottom of the window, in the bid entry, the minimum bid price will automatically appear for you. You can adjust this price manually by clicking on it and typing in your bid. When you are satisfied with your bid, click on the Bid button. The bid amount is then automatically deducted from your backpack and held by the auctioneer.

If the item has a buyout price, you can buy it immediately at that price by clicking on the Buyout button. If there is no buyout price, this button is grayed out.

Keep in mind that you cannot see the exact time remaining on an auction. Instead, the auction length field in the bid window only tells you whether the time remaining is short, medium, long, or very long.

Watching Your Bids

Once you place a bid on an item you can watch it by clicking on the Bids tab at the bottom of the auction window.

The Bids window shows all items you are currently bidding on. If you are not the highest bidder on an auction, then the name of the highest bidder is listed in red.

Getting Outbid

If you are outbid, then you will get a message on your screen and in your chat log. This message appears to you no matter where you are in the world. However, if you are outbid and wish to bid again on the item, you must return to the auction house to do so. There is no remote bidding.

Winning an Auction

If you win an auction, you are alerted to this fact in your chat log. The item you won will be waiting in your mailbox. For more information about the in-game mail system see the Post Office section of Chapter 12.

Auctioning an Item

To leave an item for sale with an auctioneer, open the Auction window by clicking on the auctioneer NPC. Click on the Auction tab at the bottom of the window. To auction an item, drag it into the auction item slot at the upper left corner of the window. A starting bid is automatically entered for you. You can adjust this price lower or higher. After you set the auction duration and are comfortable with the deposit fee, click on the Create Auction button to leave the item for sale. The item then is removed from your inventory and stays with the auctioneer.

AUCTION DURATION

After placing an item for auction and setting its starting bid, you must designate the auction's duration: two, eight, and twenty-four hours. The default duration is eight hours.

DEPOSIT FEE

When you place an auction for sale, the auctioneer requires a deposit fee that is a percentage of the starting bid price. This fee increases if the auction duration is increased beyond the default duration. Keep in mind that if you extend the duration to a longer period, the deposit fee increases. If you shorten the auction duration, the deposit fee decreases.

If the item sells, then your deposit fee is refunded to you. However, if the item does not sell in the allotted time, you lose your deposit fee.

Keep in mind that the deposit fee at the neutral auction house in Gadgetzan is much higher than the fees at the two faction-specific auction houses.

BUYOUT PRICE

At the time you set up an auction, you have the option of designating a buyout price. This is the price at which a prospective buyer could buy the item outright and end the auction. You set this price yourself.

WATCHING YOUR AUCTION

Once you leave an item for sale, it appears in the Auctions tab of the Auctions window. You can return to the auctioneer periodically to monitor your auction.

ENDING AN AUCTION

If your auction ends in a successful sale, a message in your chat log tells you your item has sold. The winning bid is then mailed to you through the game's mail system, minus the auctioneer's fee, which is a small percentage of the ultimate sale price. This is separate from the deposit fee, which is refunded to you. The auctioneer's fee is higher at Gadgetzan than it is in Ogrimmar and Ironforge.

If the auction expires and you did not sell the item, the item is returned to you through the mail, and you lose your deposit fee. The item remains in your mailbox for 30 days.

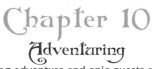

Chapter 10

Adventuring

In Azeroth, thrilling adventure and epic quests await you at every turn as you explore the world and confront legions of foes. This chapter provides more details on questing and enemies in World of Warcraft.

QUESTS

Quests are tasks set before you in the game world that you can accomplish for reward and experience.

How to Get Quests

Quests can be acquired in a variety of ways. The most common is to talk to a non-player character. NPCs that give you quests are often called quest givers.

THE EXCLAMATION POINT

You can recognize a quest giver at a glance by the yellow or silver exclamation point over its head. A yellow exclamation point means the NPC will give you a quest if you talk to him or her. A silver exclamation means the NPC has a quest for you, but you can't get the quest until you are higher level. If you hover your mouse cursor over a quest giver, the cursor will change to a chat balloon. Right-click the NPC to read the NPC's quest dialog, and then choose to either accept or decline the quest. If you accept the quest, it is penned into your quest log.

WANTED POSTERS

You can also acquire quests from wanted posters in cities. If a wanted poster has a quest for you, when you mouse over it, your cursor will change to a wheel. Right-click on the wanted poster to open up the poster's quest description. You can accept or decline the quest as you would a quest from a quest giver.

QUEST ITEMS

Quests can also be acquired from items. These items are unique and usually are looted from unique enemies. If you mouse over a unique item, and it says "This Item Begins a Quest" in the loot description, then the item will offer you a quest if you right-click it. You can accept or decline the quest as you would any other quest.

Types of Quests

There are over 2000 quests in World of Warcraft. These quests are organized into different quest types. Quests might call for you to deliver items or messages to non-player characters, to kill a given number of specific enemies, to collect loot from killed monsters, to retrieve items from unique enemies, to find and talk to other non-player characters, or to escort non-player characters to certain locations. There are more quest types than these. No matter what quest you take, the steps to complete it will be clearly outlined in the quest description. You can always open up your quest log, and reread the quest entry to see the completion requirements for the quest.

Quest Log

When you accept a quest, it appears in your quest log. Pressing the quest log tab at the bottom of the screen or pressing the hotkey L will open up the quest log. The quest log is composed of a quest list at the top of the log and a quest description at the bottom.

All your quests are organized in your quest list by the zone in which you received them. Even quests that take you to new zones will be listed in the one where you first got the quest.

You can collapse or expand the quests in each zone by clicking on the plus or minus symbol in front of each zone name. If you want to collapse all zone lists, click on the All button at the top of the quest list.

When you click on a quest in the quest list, its quest description appears. There you will find a brief synopsis of the quest; the steps needed to complete the quest; the full quest dialog; and the quest reward.

Quest Difficulty

All quests in your quest log are color coded for their relative difficulty level. The color of the quest name in your quest list tell you whether the quest is easy or hard for a character of your current level, and how much experience you can expect to earn from completing that quest.

The different colors in order from least difficult to most difficult are gray, green, yellow, orange, and red. Gray quests are for characters much lower in level than you, so they are very easy to complete and give little or no experience. Green quests are lower in level than your character is, and they are thus easy to complete on your own. They also give a fair amount of experience. Yellow quests are appropriate for a character of your level. They are more challenging than green quests, and thus give a commensurately greater experience reward. Orange quests are for characters several levels higher than yours, and should not be attempted alone. They carry a high experience reward, but are difficult to complete. Red quests are for characters many levels higher than you, and usually spell certain death for you if you attempt them by yourself. To complete orange and red quests, you should group with other players.

Completing a Quest

In each quest entry in your quest log, you will be told the objectives for completing the quest. Quests that ask you to collect items or kill monsters almost always require you to return to the NPC who gave you the quest to actually complete it. Quests that ask you to deliver a message or item end when you find the required NPC. All quests that give you a material reward usually require you to finish the quest by speaking to a non-player character so you can receive your reward.

WHERE TO TURN IN QUESTS

An easy way to tell whom you should return to in order to finish a quest is to look for a yellow question mark. When you have fulfilled all the objectives for a quest and return to an NPC to turn it in, that NPC will have a yellow question mark over its head. However, if the NPC has a gray question mark, then that means you haven't yet fulfilled all objectives. Only after you have completed all objectives will the question mark turn yellow, indicating that you can return to the NPC to finish the quest.

QUEST REWARDS

Finishing a quest will always give you a reward, whether it is a material reward, experience, or the opportunity to acquire another quest. Those quests that do offer experience usually give you a significant amount. The specific amount of experience varies from quest to quest, but a player who uses a combination of quests and monster kills to advance in level will always level up faster than a character that just kills monsters.

MATERIAL REWARDS

Some quests give you cash as a reward, while others give you items. Some quests will let you choose one reward item from a selection. These items are usually powerful equipment that is appropriate to your level. However, keep in mind that some quests will give you a material reward that is unusable by your class. In these cases, you can still sell the reward item to a merchant.

Nearly all reward items you pick up from a quest are soulbound. The exceptions are consumable reward items such as potions and food. A soulbound reward item is tied to you as soon as you acquire it so you cannot give it to another player. You can, however, sell or destroy it.

Elite Quests

Some quests have the elite tag in parentheses after their name in your quest log. These quests are much more difficult than their normal quest color indicates. These quests take place in instances, or elite dungeons, where elite monsters reside. These monsters are much stronger than normal monsters. Elite quests should be approached with caution, and should always be attempted in groups.

Abandoning Quests

You always have the option to abandon a quest that is in your quest log. Simply click on it from the quest list and then click the Abandon Quest button at the bottom of the quest log. You can always return to the quest giver to reacquire the quest at a later date.

Retrying Quests

A quest cannot be repeated once you successfully complete it. However, an abandoned quest can be reacquired if you have not yet finished it. If you fail a quest, you can always abandon it and try again.

WILDERNESS

Many of your quests will take you into the hostile wilderness between settlements. There you will find hundreds of hostile monsters, passive critters, and the occasional wandering NPC. Roads link the settlements and zones, and it is generally safe to travel along them. However, keep in mind that some monsters step onto a road from time to time while wandering.

Many quest locations and quest-related monsters can only be found deep in the wilderness, so you will often have to leave the relative safety of the road to complete quests and explore. Many resources, which are vital for trade skills, can also be found only in the wilderness. Be careful when traveling off the beaten path. Try to walk around monsters that are clearly stronger than you, or group with other players. Traveling in numbers is often safer than traveling alone.

Interacting with the Environment

As you explore the world, you will come across many objects that you can interact with. If an object can be manipulated, then when you mouse over it, your cursor will change to a different icon to reflect the action you can perform on it.

ENVIRONMENTAL QUEST OBJECTS

Some quest-related objects in the world need to be clicked to activate them. If you need to drop seeds into a fissure at the bottom of the lake to add new life to the lakebed, then your mouse cursor will change to a wheel when you mouse over the fissure. If you need to uproot timberling buds before they grow into mad timberling elementals, then your cursor will become a wheel when you mouse over the buds. These environmental objects will only be interactive if you have the quest in question. If you do not have the quest related to that object, then you will not get a wheel when you mouse over the object, and you will be unable to manipulate the object at all.

RESOURCE NODES

Many materials useful for trade skills exist in their raw forms throughout the game world. Ore for the mining skill and herbs for the herbalism skill are the two most common resource nodes in the world. If you have the appropriate skill level, right-clicking on these nodes should open up a loot window with the raw resources inside. To pick up the resources, click on them to place them in an empty bag slot. Some resource nodes can be looted multiple times before they disappear. Others can only be looted once. However, all resource nodes will replenish after a lengthy period of time, so you can always return to harvest or mine a node again.

PLACES OF INTEREST

As you explore the wilderness in each zone, you will find caves, castles, dilapidated manors, towers, and other locations to explore. These are places of interest that usually serve as focal points for quests and large gatherings of monsters.

Many of these places can be seen from above ground, but once entered reveal themselves to be composed of multiple rooms or tunnels. You can earn much experience and loot plumbing the depths of these locales. In addition, many of these places are essential end points for quests and hiding places for unique enemies.

However, you do not need a quest to enter any of these places. Some players simply explore places of interest looking for loot and experience. The monsters inside these places are usually more powerful than the monsters in the surrounding wilderness, and they are clustered in large groups. Thus, it is wise to explore places of interest with a group, unless you are much higher level than the average monsters inside.

DUNGEONS

Quite apart from places of interests are dungeons. These vast complexes of danger and challenges look at first glance to be like mundane places of interest, but inside they are many times larger and even more densely populated with enemies and monsters.

LOCATING DUNGEONS

Dungeons do not appear on your world map or minimap. You must find them on your own. Since most dungeons are destinations for quests, you should read your quest description carefully for clues to the location of the dungeon in question. You can also ask other players for help in finding the dungeon. Finally, since most dungeons are located off the beaten path, you can sometimes find them by scouring the wilderness.

INSTANCED DUNGEONS

What makes a dungeon special and different from other places of interest is the instanced portion of the dungeon. More mundane locales are small, but descend further into darkness below. However, these lengthier and more challenging sections are blocked by a swirling portal. The area of the dungeon beyond the portal is called an instance. Once you step through the instance portal, you are taken to a unique version of the dungeon that appears only for you and your adventuring group. If two

groups of adventurers entered an instance portal, each group would appear in its own instance. This enables groups in World of Warcraft to play through the most rewarding sections of a dungeon without intrusion from other players. Only the largest dungeons have an instance within them.

CORPSE RETRIEVAL IN INSTANCED DUNGEONS

Sometimes you might fall dead in the middle of an instanced dungeon. In this case, you simply need to cross through the instance portal to resurrect your body, no matter where in the instance you died. Your new body will appear just inside the instance portal.

ELITE OPPONENTS

Instances are home to elite monsters and quests, and thus are sometimes called elite dungeons as well. Within an elite dungeon, the only external indication that the monsters you are fighting are elite is the golden dragon that encircles every elite monster's NPC portrait when you click on it. These elite monsters are much stronger than other monsters of the same level, with much greater health and more powerful attacks and abilities. More so than normal adventuring locales, dungeons are almost always the final location for finding a quest NPC or quest item. The instanced portion of dungeons have even better treasure than other places, but the monsters are also commensurately stronger. Be very careful when entering an elite dungeon without help. Quests that send you to an elite dungeon have the elite tag in parentheses after the quest name in the quest log.

ENEMIES

Conflict is at the heart of the World of Warcraft. Both the Horde and the Alliance are trying to carve out a peaceful existence for themselves, but many dangers threaten to shatter this tenuous peace. Amid the oasis of stability offered by the settlements of Azeroth are ferocious monsters and hostile non-player characters.

Approaching Enemies

No matter what kind of enemy you are facing, whether it is a humanoid NPC or a monster, you can tell with a few quick clicks whether it is hostile or not to you.

If the creature or NPC you see in the world can be attacked, then your mouse cursor will change to a sword icon when you mouse over it.

If you click on an NPC or monster, three objects appear on your screen informing you about the targeted creature. There is an NPC portrait at the top of the screen, a tool tip in the bottom right of your screen, and a selection circle around the creature. If the creature is aggressive, than that means it will attack you as soon as you approach close by. You can tell if a creature is aggressive by the color of its selection circle, tool tip, and name bar in its portrait. If the color is red, then the creature is aggressive. If the color is yellow, then the creature is passive. That means that it will only attack you if you attack it first. If the color is green, then the creature or NPC is friendly and cannot be attacked. Finally, if the color is blue, then the selected target is another player character.

The tool tip will also appear whenever you mouse over a creature or NPC in the game world. Use it to your advantage to see if it is safe to approach nearby monsters and non-player characters.

Hostile NPCs

Non-player characters that might be friendly to one faction of players aren't so friendly to others. NPCs in the Horde lands are hostile to Alliance players, and Alliance NPCs are hostile to Horde players. Be careful when approaching such hostile non-player characters. The Horde and Alliance are not allies.

Enemy Type

There are many types of monsters in the World of Warcraft. They are all grouped into several categories, or types. Sample types include beasts, undead, demons, dragons, and humanoids. The type of monster is important because certain spells and talents are designed to affect only certain monster types. For example, beast slaying is an enchantment that you can place on a weapon that gives you a +2 damage bonus against all beast monsters, which include lions, raptors, bears, and spiders.

You can tell what type the creature is by clicking on it. In the tool tip, after the creature's name and level, you will see its type displayed.

Enemy Level

Finding out if an enemy will attack you on sight or only attack in self-defense is your first step in determining how to approach that enemy. You also have to discover the strength of your enemy. Fighting monsters that are much higher in level than you is dangerous, as you will likely die.

The tool tip and NPC portrait of a targeted monster also tells you the level of the monster selected. If the level of the monster in the tool tip is displayed as a skull and crossbones, then that means the monster is far beyond your level. You will not survive a battle against this enemy.

Keep in mind also that battle against higher-level foes is riskier not just because they have increased health and attack, but also because they have a greater chance to resist your spells and abilities.

Monsters are much deadlier when they fight in numbers, so even two opponents of the same level as you might be too strong to overcome. How many monsters you can defeat in battle also depends on your class and your skill.

Tagging Enemies

Once you attack a monster, you effectively tag it. That means you mark it as your opponent and only you will earn experience and the right to loot it if you kill it. Tagging prevents other players from swooping in at the last minute to kill your foe and steal its loot. You can tell if a monster is tagged by clicking on it and then looking at its name bar in the NPC portrait. If the color is gray, then the monster is tagged. If it is its normal color (red or yellow depending on its aggressiveness) then it is not tagged.

Status Conditions

During battle, many conditions might affect your character. You could be stunned and unable to take any actions; poisoned or diseased, and thus suffering from constant damage over time; feared and thus forced to flee battle; or cursed and weakened in some way. In contrast to the friendly buffs you or your party members cast on you, these afflictions are outlined in red to show their harmful nature.

You can mouse over these icons to see what these conditions do and how long they will last.

Enemy Pop-up Text

During battles, much of the pertinent information in your combat log will also pop up over your target's head. This is a quick and easy way to see how the battle is progressing.

Damage you deal from weapon attacks and direct damage spells is shown as a white number over the opponent's head. Damage you deal over time, though spells, abilities, and items, is shown as a yellow number.

If the opponent resists or is immune to your attack, a white "resist" or "immune" appears over its head when you attack. Defensive abilities that also deal damage back at the attacker, such as damage shields, are also considered attacks. Thus, the enemy might have an attack-related message over their head even if you didn't explicitly attack it because of your damage shield.

Any time your opponent dodges or blocks an attack, it will also be displayed in white letters above its head.

Portrait Information

Your character portrait displays the same information during a fight that you see over your opponent's head, but tailored for your character. Thus, any damage your opponent deals to you appears as white numbers over your character portrait. Damage over time to you appears as yellow numbers. If you dodge, resist, block, absorb, or are immune to an attack, that fact also appears over your portrait. If you heal yourself, the amount of healing appears in green numbers over your portrait.

Your health, mana, energy, and rage bars also fluctuate to show how much health you are losing and gaining in battle, and how much mana, energy, or rage you are using.

If you have any pets, the same information also appears in their portraits during battle. You cannot see actual health, mana, energy, and rage numbers for any party members you are grouped with.

Watch your combat log and character portrait closely to monitor your status in battle, healing yourself or adjusting your strategy as necessary to keep yourself alive and achieve victory.

Looting Enemies

Once you kill a monster, it leaves behind a corpse or pile of goods you can loot. If you mouse over a lootable corpse or fallen items, your mouse cursor will change to a purse. Right-click on the corpse or remains to open the loot window.

Loot Window

The loot window shows any treasure, or loot, on the corpse. The loot window has room for four items. If there are more than four items on the corpse, you can scroll to the next page to see the extra treasure. To loot the corpse, click on the items in the loot window and they are automatically placed in your inventory. Clicking on coins likewise adds them to your backpack.

When all items have been looted, the loot window closes and the corpse can no longer be looted. If you leave an item on the corpse, you can return to it later to loot it.

You can only loot a corpse that you tagged and killed. If you are in a party, depending on the loot system set by your party leader, you might have to wait your turn to loot, or you might be able to loot any monster killed by anyone in your party. More information about party looting can be found in the Community chapter.

Corpse Decay

A corpse slowly decays over time. You should loot corpses right away. If you wait too long, they will eventually disappear, even if they still have treasure left on them.

Quest-related Enemies

Many quests call for you to kill a certain number of enemies. Simply killing them is sufficient to complete the quest.

Other quests ask you to loot items off specific monsters' corpses. When this is the case, the monsters will only drop those items if you have the appropriate quest. When you then go to loot those monsters, the needed items will occasionally appear in their loot window in addition to the treasure you would normally find. If you do not have the quest, then the monsters will simply drop regular loot.

Certain quests ask you to bring back a unique character's body part or possession, such as an arm, head, book, or ring. In these cases, after killing the unique character, its body part or possession will appear in the loot window.

If you are in a group with other players, you will have to wait your turn when collecting quest-necessary items from monster corpses. However, if you are on a quest to retrieve a unique character's body part or possession, it will be available for looting from all party members. The unique character's corpse will remain lootable until all party members have taken the necessary item or until the corpse decays as normal. However, as with normal group rules, if a party member was not near the unique character and did not participate in killing it, then that party member cannot loot the unique character's corpse.

Chapter 11
Horde Versus Alliance

The war between the Horde and Alliance has been at the core of the Warcraft mythos for years. Recently, a ceasefire was agreed upon by the Horde chief Thrall and the Alliance leader Jaina Proudmoore, but the fact remains that animosity is still high between the two factions. In some places, this undercurrent of hostility has erupted into open warfare.

In World of Warcraft, the tension between the factions is reflected in the player versus player game system. Players from different factions can attack each other and continue the race war between Horde and Alliance through their in-game skirmishes.

Player Versus Player Combat

Under certain conditions, you can fight players of the opposing faction. You cannot fight players in your own faction, except through duels. Duels are explained later in this chapter.

Player versus player (PvP) combat is similar to normal combat against monsters. However, there are some key differences.

You cannot attack other players at will. Certain conditions must be met first before you can begin PvP combat. These conditions are easier to meet on servers designated as PvP servers, and harder to meet on PvE servers.

Level differences are less important. Although your damage per second, health, mana, and available abilities are better if you are higher level, all other combat factors are equal when playing other players. For example, your chance to dodge, block, or resist spells is the same whether you fight a level-one player or a level-sixty player. This makes the playing field fairer for players of differing level, while still maintaining a sizeable advantage for players with a great level advantage.

Spells are limited against other players. Against monsters, your crowd control spells – those spells that incapacitate or control the target - operate normally. However, against other players, your spells are subject to diminished returns. On your first casting these spells have 100 percent of their effect, but on subsequent castings against the same target, these spells have 75 percent effect, then 50 percent effect, and finally zero effect. Spells subject to this rule include those that control or limit other players, such as polymorph, fear, and stun.

Server Types

There are two different kinds of servers: Normal servers and PvP servers. Before you create a character, you first must decide what server type you want to play on. This decision determines how hard or easy it will be to fight other players in the game. The conditions for enabling player versus player combat are different depending on where you play.

Choosing a Server

If you want the thrill of fighting other players, and prefer the challenge of player-controlled opponents over computer-controlled ones, then the PvP server is for you. However, if you choose this server, be aware that in most areas of the world you risk getting attacked by higher-level enemy players when you least expect it. Not only might they be too powerful for you, but they'll also strike when you are at your most vulnerable. For example, they might attack you while you are in the middle of a quest or a monster fight. Interference by opposing players is a constant reality you must accept on a PvP server.

If you want to restrict your gameplay to computer-controlled challenges, and want the freedom to enter PvP mode only at your own choosing, then the PvE server is for you.

NORMAL SERVER

On the normal server, PvP mode is disabled by default. You have to turn it on through your own actions. When you enable PvP mode, you turn on a flag that other players can see. On your own character portrait, you will see a PvP flag next to your face that looks like a shield belonging to your faction. Other players will also see this, and they will be able to attack you at will. You can enable this flag by doing any of the following:

- Attacking an NPC of an opposing faction, such as the opposing faction's aerial mount master, guards, quest giver, vendor, or similar NPC.

- Attacking an opposing player that attacked a friendly NPC. By counter-attacking the first player, you enable PvP mode, and opposing players can begin attacking you.

- Aiding a player engaged in PvP combat.

- Entering an enemy capital city.

Besides these four ways, you can also type /pvp at the cha
prompt to enable PvP mode. In all cases, other players can onl
attack you if you enable the PvP flag through your own action
You always have control over whether opposing players can attac
you or not on a PvE server. That means PvP is consensual-only o
normal servers.

Turning Off PvP Mode

On the normal server, PvP mode lasts five minutes. At that time
you revert back to your default non-PvP mode. However, if yo
engage in any of the above PvP-enabling actions, this timer wi
reset to five minutes.

Player Versus Player Server

On a player versus player server, there are additional conditions tha
enable PvP mode. You can enable PvP mode by doing the following

♦ Entering an enemy territory.

♦ Entering a contested territory.

♦ Attacking another player.

♦ Attacking an opposing NPC.

♦ Aiding a player engaged in PvP combat.

Territory Control

On a PvP server, all zones are divided into three categories: friendly
contested, and enemy. The concept of territory control allow
low-level players a measure of security in their home zones, bu
also heightens the risk and danger of venturing into farther-reachin
areas beyond the protection of their faction guards.

Friendly Territories: You are safe from opposing players whil
you are in friendly territory unless you attack those players
While the territory is friendly for you, remember that the sam
territory is considered enemy territory for the opposing playe
Based on the PvP rules, you can attack enemy players wh
come into your friendly zones, but doing so can be unwis
because they can only attack you if you attack them first.

Contested Territories: Contested territories are neutral ground
and thus any player in these areas can be attacked by any opposin
players. By definition, contested territories are dangerous, and
all players are fair game as long as they remain here.

Enemy Territories: In enemy territories, opposing players ca
attack you at will, but you cannot attack them unless they attac
first or enable PvP in some other way.

Battlegrounds

Battlegrounds are a special type of zone where unique player versus player challenges can be found. They exist on both PvE and PvP servers, and provide a level of competitive inter-faction play that can't be found anywhere else.

Battlegrounds are special areas distinguished by a red instance portal. The first time you encounter a battleground, you must walk through this red portal to enter it, although later, you can journey there via flying mount if you unlock the flight path there.

In a battleground, player versus player combat is always enabled, regardless of server type. This gives players on the PvE server who want a taste of PvP gameplay the ability to do so on more manageable terms.

While in a battlegrounds area, you can team up with friendly players while you embark on quests designed to pit you against players of the opposing faction.

You can easily leave a battlegrounds area and return to the normal world by speaking to another friendly battleground NPC.

PvP Messages

You can get an update of player versus player action on a local and global scale through the Local Defense and World Defense chat channels. By default, these chat channels are turned off, but you can turn them on by typing "/join localdefense" and "/join worlddefense" at the chat prompt. You can also turn off these channels by typing "/leave localdefense" and "/leave worlddefense".

When these channels are turned on, a "zone under attack" message appears in your chat log any time an opposing player attacks a friendly NPC in the mentioned zone.

This tells you where enemy players are acting so you can confront them if you so desire.

PLAYER VERSUS PLAYER REWARDS

The thrill and challenge of fighting other players are usually reward
enough for the first few battles, but there are significant incentive
to make continued PvP battles worthwhile.

HONOR POINTS

As you kill opposing players and special PvP-enabling non-playe
characters, you will earn honor points. You also gain honor point
for conquering contested battlegrounds and slaying importan
NPCs such as leaders and generals of the opposing faction. At th
end of each day, these honor points will be distributed to all player
who participated in PvP gameplay, with players contributing th
most kills for their side earning the most points. These hono
points accumulate to give you a PvP rank, which can fluctuat
based on your participation and success in PvP play.

DISHONOR POINTS

Even among enemies as bitter as the Horde and Alliance, there i
honor. If you flaunt this honor and engage in objectionable Pv
play, such as killing new players vastly inferior to you in level, o
killing essential non-combat NPCs such as flight masters or ques
givers, you will earn dishonor. If you accumulate enough dishono
through your criminal actions, you will be branded an outlaw. A:
a consequence, you'll suffer experience penalties, lose access to
your own faction cities, and become so hated by even your own
kind that every faction NPC will attack you on sight.

RECOVERING DISHONOR

World of Warcraft is forgiving of transgressions, and if you refrain
from dishonorable actions for a long enough time, you will eventually
return to favor with your faction and cast off your criminal label.

REWARDS

In addition to an honor score, your PvP successes will also enable
you to acquire a high rank and title, earn special reward items
and gain access to special buildings and merchants. You'll also
gain the favor of your faction's leadership, and earn other rewards
that are unavailable to players who refrain from PvP play.

The honor system and PvP rewards exist on both normal and PvP
servers, but the incentives for player versus player gameplay on
the PvP servers are higher due to the very nature of the server.

More details on the risks, rewards, and consequences of playe
versus player gameplay are available at the World of Warcraf
strategy site at **http://www.worldofwarcraft.com**.

DUELS

While player versus player gameplay is perfectly viable and rewarding, there is a means of friendlier competition that isn't as intense as faction versus faction violence. If you wish to test your skill against other players, you can challenge them to a duel.

ISSUING A CHALLENGE

A duel challenge can be issued on a PvP or non-PvP server. To challenge a player to a duel, select the player and then right-click on the player's portrait. Select the Duel option. The other player can then either accept or decline the challenge.

When a challenge is first issued, a duel flag drops down between the two players, signaling to other players that a duel is about to commence. If the other player declines the duel, the duel flag disappears. If the other player accepts, then the duel is on, and the flag continues to wave until a winner emerges.

As soon as the other player consents to the duel, you and the other player can begin attacking each other, using the same abilities, spells, and tactics you employ against the monsters you normally fight against.

Note

> When one player is reduced to zero health, the duel is over, and the winner is the surviving player.
>
> You also win the duel if the other player strays too far from the duel flag, thus forfeiting the match.

CONCLUDING A DUEL

You do not have to worry about losing experience, dying, or being looted if you lose a duel. However, you also don't gain experience or treasure for defeating another player in a duel. Instead, a duel is just a friendly test of combat skill. You can duel players within your faction or in the opposite faction.

Chapter 12
Community

World of Warcraft is a game built on community. There are hundreds of other players from around the world playing this game alongside you, and interacting with them is as much a part of the game as hunting monsters and finding treasure.

You can talk to other players through chat or in-game mail. You can trade with other players through the trade channel or auction houses. You can also group with other players for help and company on quests.

For more lasting relationships with the community, you can also form in-game friendships and join a guild.

Additional information can be found at the World of Warcraft community page at **http://www.worldofwarcraft.com**.

CHATTING

Your window for chatting is your chat log, which is located in the lower left area of your screen, above the Action Bar. Chapter 3, Getting Started has information on the basic controls for using the chat log. This section goes into greater detail about using chat to communicate with other players in the game.

Channels

The messages displayed in your chat log are from all chat channels you have joined in the current zone. A number and channel name in brackets precede every chat message. The name is the chat channel that the message originated from, and the hotkey number corresponds to that channel. By default, whenever you enter a zone, you automatically join the zone's General and Trade channels.

To see a list of all channels in the zone, type /chatlist.

JOINING AND LEAVING CHANNELS

To join a chat channel, type /join followed by the name of the chat channel. For example: /join trade.

To leave a channel, type /leave followed by the name of the channel you wish to exit. For example: /leave general.

CREATING A CHANNEL

To create a channel, type /join followed by the name of the channel you wish to create. If no channel by that name exists, one will be created for you. Others can then join your channel with the join command.

136

Chat Modes

There are different types of chat. Pressing the Chat Button next to the chat log shows you these different options. Simply click on the desired chat type to begin chatting in that manner, whether it is yelling, guild chatting, or whispering. You can also bypass the Chat Button by pressing the Enter key to pull up the chat prompt and then typing / followed by the appropriate chat command or hotkey.

/SAY

Say broadcasts your chat to all players in your vicinity. This is the default chat mode. You can also type /s at the chat prompt to begin saying a message if your chat prompt is set to a different chat type.

/PARTY

Party chat only chats with members of your party. Use this chat to speak with your party members without cluttering the chat window of other players. You can also type /p to begin a party message.

/GUILD

Guild chat broadcasts a message to all people in your guild, no matter where they are. You can also type /g to begin a guild message.

/YELL

Yell broadcasts a message to all players in your zone. The chat message appears red by default in everyone's chat window, making it stand out. You can also type /y to yell a message.

/WHISPER

Whispering sends a private message to one player. Unlike other chat types, you must specify a player to whisper to. After clicking the whisper command or typing /w at the chat prompt, type the name of the player you wish to whisper to. Then type your message. Whispers cannot be sent to players in the opposing faction.

/TELL

A tell is functionally equivalent to a whisper. Both send a private message to a single player. You can also send a tell by typing /t followed by your message. Tells cannot be sent to players in the opposing faction.

/REPLY

If a player sends you a whisper or tell, you can reply to that player either by choosing Reply from the Chat Button menu or by pressing r.

Chat Memory

By default, when you hit the Enter key to pull up the chat prompt, your chat will be a /say message. However, if you send a different type of chat, such as "/party," the next time you pull up your chat prompt, you will still be in party chat mode. The chat prompt remembers your last chat mode and stays there until you specify a new one.

Other Chat Commands

Chat usually refers to typed messages, but you can also communicate in other ways through the chat prompt.

LOOKING FOR PLAYERS? /WHO

The who command lets you look for other players that are online. To use it, open the chat prompt and type /who [playername]. If the player is on, the who command will display the player's character name, level, race, class, guild affiliation, and current zone in your chat log. If the player is not online, you will see a "0 players total" message.

You can also use the /who command to look for multiple players in a zone or guild. If your guild name is Blizzard, typing /who Blizzard will show you all players with Blizzard in their names or in their guild names. You can see all the players currently in a zone by typing /who [zone name].

If the list includes more than eight players, the who command will instead open the who list in the Social Window.

/EMOTE

Emoting isn't technically a form of chat. Instead, emoting is a way for your character to perform an action or display emotion in the chat log. To emote, open the chat prompt and type the appropriate emote, such as /thank, /cheer, or /dance. A text message saying what emote you are performing will then appear in your chat log, as well as in the chat logs of nearby players.

Many emotes are also accompanied by an animation that your character performs. For example, if you perform the cheer emote while playing an orc character, the chat log will say [Playername] cheers, while your character pumps both fists jubilantly in the air. Other races might cheer differently, but your character would still act it out in the game.

If you select a player or NPC when you emote, you will perform the emote to that target, provided the emote can have a target. If you have nothing selected or the emote doesn't allow a target, you will perform the emote to the general public.

A partial list of over 100 emotes can be found online at
http://www.worldofwarcraft.com/info/basics/emotes.shtml.

Speech

Speech is a list of common phrases that you will say during the course of adventuring. For convenience, these phrases are reduced to simple speech commands that your character actually voices in the game. There are over a dozen pre-set speech phrases. To use them, select on Speech from the Chat Button and then click on the desired speech. You can also type /v and the desired speech command at the chat prompt. Speech is a way to communicate a complex situation quickly without typing a long message. If you need healing right away, simply type /v heal, and your character will say a plea for healing.

Language

By default, all Alliance races chat in Common, and all Horde races chat in Orcish. However, you can switch to your racial language when chatting by selecting a different language via Language from the Chat Button. When you speak your faction's default language, such as Orcish for Horde players, only members of your faction can read your speech. Language is a toggle and does not have to be specified each time you type a message.

Ignoring Players

As with any community, there are rude and annoying people. If you find someone's chat messages offensive, you can place that player on your ignore list so that none of that player's messages appear in your chat log. As long as a person is on your ignore list, you will never see any of their messages, whether they are in general chat, mail, or private tells.

To ignore someone, type /ignore [playername] at the chat prompt or open up the ignore list in your Social Window (hotkey O), and click the Ignore Player button. You will then be prompted to type in the player's name.

You can remove a player from your ignore list by typing /ignore [playername] a second time at the chat prompt, or by selecting the player and clicking the "Remove Player" button from the ignore list.

Inspecting Players

You can inspect another player by selecting the player, right-clicking on the player's portrait, and then choosing the Inspect action. This opens up a character window of the targeted player. You can see that character, as well as all items equipped and held by the character. Mousing over an object in this window opens up the info box with the item's relevant stats.

GROUPING

You don't have to adventure alone in World of Warcraft. In fact, the game can be more fun when you join with other players. Quests that are too difficult alone can be surprisingly easy to accomplish when you group with other players. If you group with other players frequently enough, they might even become regular adventuring companions and friends.

Creating a Group

A group, or party, of adventurers can have a maximum of five players. A group is created as soon as one other player joins you. You can invite a player to join your group in three ways.

♦ You can select the player, right-click on the player's portrait, and select the invite command from the resulting dropdown menu.

♦ You can type the /invite command followed by the player's name at your chat prompt.

♦ You can add the player to your friends list, then select that player from your friends list in the Social window and click the Group Invite button.

Players you can see next to you can be invited by any of these three means. However, players that you cannot see, usually because they are far away or in a different zone, must be invited through the /invite command or through the Group Invite button on the friends list.

A player already in another group cannot join your group. If you extend an invitation to such a player, you will get a message back saying the other person is already in a group.

Joining a Group

If you are adventuring by yourself and are invited into a group, you can accept or decline the invitation. However, if you are already in a group, then you will be unable to join a new group until you leave your current group.

Party Leader

By default, the person who made the first invite is the party leader. Only the party leader can extend subsequent invites to other players to fill out the remaining spots in a group. The party leader is also the only member of the group that can change the looting system, remove players from a group, and select a new leader.

Removing a Member of the Party

To remove a player from the group, the party leader must select the party member and then right-click on his or her portrait. Select the Uninvite option to remove that player from the group. A party leader should not use this feature capriciously. Generally, differences in your party should be worked out through civil conversation first. Removing a player should be a last resort. However, if you are grouped with a player who is abusive and violates the Terms of Use agreement, then you remove the player from your group and report the objectionable behavior to a GM.

Selecting a New Party Leader

If you wish to abdicate your leadership role and select a new party member to be leader, select that player and then right-click on that player's portrait. Choose the Promote to leader option to make them party leader.

If the current party leader leaves the group, the next player in the lineup automatically becomes the leader.

Group Rules

When you join a group, several aspects of adventuring change for your character. Loot and experience must be shared among the members of the group.

Shared Experience

Experience is usually evenly divided among all players in the group. In cases of level disparities among the group members, each individual member might get a different amount of experience depending on that member's level, but no one player gets more by doing more or less work in the group.

An exception to the evenly divided experience occurs when a party member is not near the group. If the party attacks and kills a monster, all party members nearby will gain experience. Any party members too far away to see the attack will not get any experience.

Level Disparity

Experience awards for killing a monster will be equal when the party members are all the same level, but if there is a disparity in the levels of the group, then each member will get a different amount of experience.

World of Warcraft calculates your experience based on a variety of factors, including your level, the level of the monster, and your level relative to the rest of the party and the monster killed.

The total experience for a kill is then divided among the party members, with the higher-level members getting a bigger share of the experience. However, if the disparity is small, the difference in experience rewards is minimal.

However, if the highest-level party member is much higher in level than the monster killed, that player will not get experience, and in turn, no one in the party will get experience.

While it can sometimes be beneficial to have higher-level players in your group to help you fight monsters, they can reduce your experience reward. Thus, try to group with players close to your level.

Group Looting

There are three looting systems in a group. The default system is round robin. Only the party leader can change the looting system.

Round Robin: Players take turns looting the monsters killed by the party. When a monster is killed, one player in the group is allowed to loot that monster. When the next monster is killed, the next player is allowed to loot. This continues until the first player's turn occurs again, and looting continues to pass among the members of the group.

Free For All: There are no turns or waiting. When a monster dies, it can be looted by anyone in the party. The first one to reach the dead monster gets the loot.

Master Looter: In this loot system, only the party leader can loot kills. It is then the party leader's responsibility to distribute loot to the rest of the group.

Looting Quest Items

Some quests are collection requests that require you to collect quest items off the bodies of dead monsters. These items are considered normal loot, so you must wait your turn to get them if using the round robin system. This type of quest item is often called a single loot item, because it can only be looted by one player.

However, there are some quests that ask you to bring back a specific quest item from a unique character, such as an NPC's head or a stolen item. These are bounty quests, and the quest item you need is a group loot item, meaning it will spawn multiple copies of itself so that every party member can pick it up. You can even loot this item when it isn't your turn in round robin. No matter what loot system is in effect, the corpse and the group loot item will stay up so that everyone in the party can loot it. The exception to this rule is that if you were not in the vicinity when the monster was killed, you cannot loot the group loot quest item from it.

The game does not tell you which quest items are group loots and which are not. However, in general, a quest item from a unique enemy character tends to be a group loot, while a quest item from a non-unique monster tends to be a single loot. The head of Edwin VanCleef is a group-loot item, while Bloodscalp troll ears are single-loot items. The former is a drop from a unique NPC, while the latter are drops from non-unique monsters.

Leaving a Group

Leaving a group is easy. You can simply right-click on your character portrait and select Leave party from the menu options. You might also leave a group because the party leader has removed you from it. If this happens, send a private message to the party leader. You might have been removed as a mistake. If this is not the case, it usually is not worth the trouble to ask to be re-invited. Make sure you remember the player who slighted you, though, so you don't bother grouping with them again.

Whom to Group With

Group with players who are close to your level and who have the same quests you do. While you can group with any player, having too wide a level disparity among the group can severely limit the experience you gain from killing monsters. Also, if you aren't all working towards the same quests, then grouping might not be the most efficient use of every group member's time.

Keep track of players that you group with. If you have a good time with them, and find that they are pleasant company, you might want to adventure together again, especially if they are fair in distributing treasure and democratic in determining what quests to undertake.

If you would like to group with these players again, add them to your friends list so you can track when they are online.

Conversely, if you don't like the people you group with, don't group with them again. Particularly offensive players can be added to your ignore list so you aren't bothered by them again.

TRADING

In the course of playing the game, you might have occasion to trade with other players, whether to give items to friends, receive items in kind, or participate in buying and selling of items with other players.

Trading between two players is a simple operation. To make a trade, you can right-click on another player and select the "Trade" choice from the menu, or you can take the item you wish to trade and drag it onto the other player.

When this happens, a Trade window appears on the screen.

Trade Window

The trade window displays two halves – one for each player – split into seven slots. Six of the slots are for trading. You can place one item or stack of items within each of these slots, which means you can trade a total of six slots worth of items to another player. To place an item for trade, drag it into an empty slot in your half. The seventh slot is for items that will not be traded, but that can be acted upon by the other player. For instance, if you find a lockbox that you want a friendly rogue to unlock for you, you can place it in this seventh slot and the rogue can unlock it from there. This prevents you from having to trade the lockbox first and then having the rogue trade it back to you.

Offering Money for Trade

To drag money into the Trade Window, left-click on your cash in your backpack (hotkey B or F12). To grab gold, click on the gold; to grab silver, click on the silver; and to grab copper, click on the copper. A small window pops up where you type in the amount of money you want to trade. Your cursor then turns into a coin icon with the cash you specified. Drag it into an empty slot in the Trade Window. It then appears in the money field just above your six slots.

Completing a Trade

When the buyer and seller are both happy with the items and cash offered in the trade window, both must click the Trade button for the trade to be completed.

Canceling a Trade

To cancel a trade, hit the Cancel button in the Trade Window or press the Esc key.

FRIENDS

You will eventually find players that you enjoy talking to and grouping with. You can make them friends so it is easier for you to meet with them online. The friends list in your Social window (hotkey O), shows you a list of all your friends in the game. You can add a friend to your friends list by opening the chat prompt and typing /invite [playername] or by clicking the Add Friend button on the friends list and typing the player's name.

All your friends are listed on your friends page. Each friend entry shows you whether the friend is online or offline, and displays that friend's name, level, class, and current location.

Anytime a friend logs on or off the game, you get a message in your chat log telling you that the friend has come online or gone offline. You can also easily invite your friends to a group, regardless of where they are, by clicking the Group Invite button on the friends list.

GUILDS

A guild is a collection of players who have joined together to create a mutually beneficial relationship with each other. Many guilds are created by people who are friends outside the game, while other guilds are created by players who have become friends in the game and want to pool their resources together.

Guild Benefits

Being in a guild carries many benefits. Few of these benefits are dictated by the game; instead, these benefits arise because friends gathered together in a guild are already inclined to help each other out.

Guild members benefit each other by loaning or giving cash to each other, by trading items to each other for little or no charge, and by donating equipment to each other.

Many guilds also set up an efficient structure for improving trade skill use. Some members become gatherers, while other members specialize in a trade skill. The gatherers then feed the specialists raw materials so they can improve their trade skill more quickly than normal and thus make better equipment for the entire guild.

Being in a guild also means you have ready allies to group with you if you need help on quests.

Guild Tabard

One tangible benefit of being in a guild is the ability to wear a guild tabard. Players who are not in a guild cannot place any item in the tabard slot of their character.

The guild leader must first create a crest design to go on the tabard. You can do that by speaking to a Guild Master NPC. Most guild leaders solicit input from guild officers or the entire guild when designing the tabard. A crest design, once created, cannot be changed.

Once the guild leader has designed a crest design for the guild tabard, the guild leader must pay 10 gold to solidify the design and make the tabard available for guild members to purchase. Although this is a lot of cash, many guilds take donations from all guild members to pay this cost.

After the crest has been designed and purchased, any guild member can go to a Guild Tabard Vendor NPC and buy a tabard. A tabard costs one gold piece, but for that price you get a prestigious symbol of your guild allegiance.

Creating a Guild

In order to create a guild, you must have a minimum of 10 starting guild members. One of these players must be the guild leader.

The guild leader must find a Guild Master NPC in a city and purchase a guild charter from that NPC for 10 silver. The guild leader must then get nine other players to sign the guild charter. After 10 people are on the charter, it must be returned to a Guild Master NPC and registered.

Naming Your Guild

When you purchase your charter, you must name your guild. Have several choices ready, since your first guild name might already be taken.

Guilds must adhere to the same naming policy as player character names. That means the guild name must be inoffensive and appropriate. Guild names that promote or refer to racial, ethnic, religious, or gender discrimination in any form will not be tolerated. Other inappropriate guild names include those that refer to extreme violence, obscenities, drug use, or that insult specific players or people. Any guild found to have an inappropriate name will be contacted by a GM. In some cases, the guild will be asked to rename itself. In extreme cases, a guild will be disbanded.

Guild Ranks

There are various ranks in a guild. From lowest rank to highest rank, they are initiate, member, veteran, officer, and leader. There can only be one guild leader at a time.

Both the guild leader and guild officers can add or remove players from the guild. Only the guild leader can disband the guild or promote guild members to officer status.

When you first join a guild, you automatically enter as an initiate. To move up in rank, you must be promoted by the guild leader.

Each individual guild has its own method of deciding when and how to promote members. However, technically, the guild leader simply needs to press the "Promote" button on the Guild page in the Social Window.

The Guild Page

In the Social Window (hotkey O), there is a Guild tab. If you belong to a guild, you can click that tab to call up the Guild page. This is the place where the guild leader and officers can manage the guild, and where other members can view guild information.

Member List

The member list dominates your Guild page. It lists the names of every guild member, as well as their current zone, level, and class. Below this list is a button you can click to view guild status. Clicking on that button changes the list to display each member's rank and last time online instead of each member's level and class. The bottom of the member list also tells you how many guild members are currently online.

Guild Management

At the bottom of the Guild page are buttons to promote, demote, remove, and add guild members. Only officers and leaders can use these buttons. They are grayed out to all other members of the guild.

Additional Guild Information

For more details on how to manage a guild, visit the World of Warcraft strategy site at **http://www.worldofwarcraft.com**.

POSTAL SERVICE

Communicating face-to-face is the preferred method of communication, but for those occasions when your friend guildmate, or another player isn't around for an immediate conversation, you can turn to the World of Warcraft Postal Service With it, you can send mail, money, and packages to other players Mail and packages can only be sent to players in your faction.

To send mail or packages, you must find a mailbox and ther right-click on it. Mailboxes are usually located near inns in the game, and in some cases by banks. Clicking on the mailbox opens the Mail Window.

Inbox

Your Mail Window has two pages. The first page is your inbox where any messages or packages will be waiting for you. There is no limit to the number of messages or packages you can have in your inbox at a time. However, messages left in your inbox past a certain amount of time will expire.

Opening Mail

To open mail, just left-click on the message. The mail will open on your screen, and any items or money sent with the message will also appear there.

Replying to Mail

To reply to a message, click on the Reply button. This automatically opens up the Send page and fills in the sender's name as the receiver of your reply.

Send Mail

The second page in your Mail Window is the Send Mail page. You can move between the pages by clicking on the corresponding tabs at the bottom of the Mail Window.

You can send three types of mail: normal mail, packages, and C.O.D. (Cash On Delivery) packages. To specify the type of mail you wish to send, click the appropriate circle at the bottom of the Send Mail page. Sending any type of mail costs 30 copper per message.

Regular Mail

Regular mail consists of a text message. You must type the name of the player in the To field. Your regular mail can consist of a subject and a written message. You can also send money with your regular mail. This type of mail is sent instantaneously to the receiver.

Packages

To send a package, simply drag an item from your inventory into the package slot at the bottom of the Send page. Doing this automatically turns a regular mail delivery into a package mail delivery. A package takes one hour to arrive at the receiver's inbox. You can only attach one item to each message, so to send multiple items, you must send multiple messages.

C.O.D. Packages

A C.O.D. package must be paid for by the receiver. If the receiver accepts the charge, then that player can open the message and take the item as normal. The receiver has the option to refuse to pay for the package by clicking the "Return" button, which sends the item back to the sender. The receiver can also postpone payment to a later date. However, the item will not release to the sender until payment has been made.

Expiring Mail

Mail sitting in your inbox will eventually expire. Regular mail and packages stays in your inbox for 30 days, at which point they are deleted. C.O.D. packages stay in your inbox for 3 days. After 3 days, the message expires, and the item is returned to the sender.

Northern Kalimdor

Teldrassil
Shadow Glen
Darnassus
Rut'theran Village

Moonglade
Starfall
Blackfathom Deeps
Nighthaven
Darkshore
Winterspring
Talonbranch Glade
Auberdine
Felwood
Everlook
World Tree
Mount Hyjal
Bloodvenom Post
Ruins of Eldarath
Hetaera Clutch
Astranaar
Kargathia Outpost
Azshara
Stonetalon Peak
Ashenvale
Orgrimmar
Stonetalon Mountains
Durotar
Nigel's Point
Sunrock Retreat
The Barrens
Valley of Trials
Thunder Bluff
Desolace
The Crossroads
Ratchet
Mulgore
Jagged Spear Village
Camp Narache
Camp Taurajo

Southern Kalimdor

Desolace
Oneiros

Mulgore

The Barrens
Brackenwall Village

Theramore

Feralas

Camp Mojache

Dustwallow Marsh

Feathermoon Stronghold

Thousand Needles

Freewind Post

Shimmering Flats

Marshal's Refuge

Zul'farrak

Un'goro Crater

Fire Plume Ridge

Gadgetzan

Silithus

Tanaris

Ahn'qiraj

Lordaeron

SUNWELL GROVE

SILVERMOON

QUEL'THALAS

MAISARA HILLS

TIRISFAL GLADES

STRATHOLME

ZUL'AMAN

HEARTHGLEN

BRILL

W. PLAGUELANDS

SHRIN OF ULA'

DEATHKNELL

THE SEPULCHER

ANDORHAL

CAER DARROW

E. PLAGUELANDS

THE UNDERCITY

TYR'S HAND

ALTERAC

SILVERPINE

FENRIS ISLE

AERIE PEAK

SHADOWFANG KEEP

ALTERAC MTNS.

HINTERLANDS

AMBERMILL

PYREWOOD

DALARAN

TARREN MILL

THE GREYMANE WALL

HILLSBRAD

STROMGARDE

HILLSBRAD FOOTHILLS

SOUTH SHORE

ARATHI HIGHLANDS

GILNEAS

TOL BARAD

THE THANDOL SPAN

DUN MODR

ZUL'DARE

THE WETLANDS

DRAGONMAW GATES

CRESTFALL

GRIM BATOL

ALGAZ GATE

MENETHIL HARBOR

STONEWROUGHT DAM

FARSTRIDER'S LODGE

IRONFORGE

KUL TIRAS

GNOMEREGAN

KHARANOS

LOCH MODAN

DUN MOROGH

THELSAMAR

EXCAVATION SITE

COLDRIDGE VALLEY

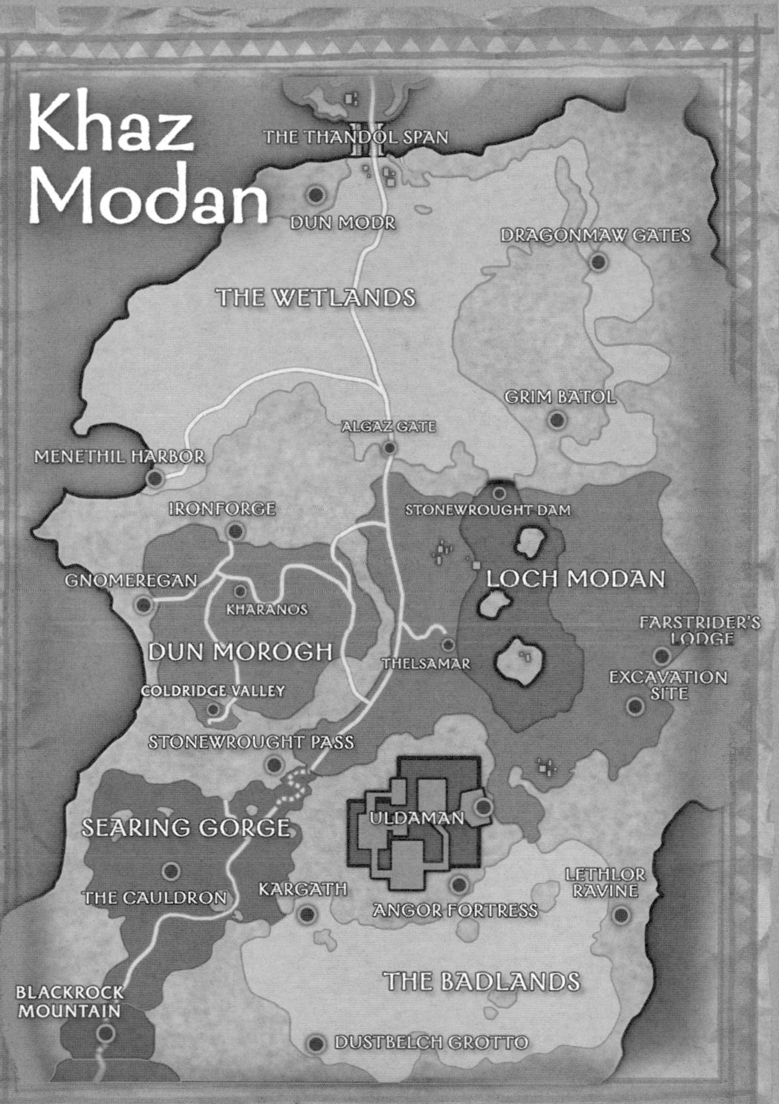

Khaz Modan

THE THANDOL SPAN

DUN MODR

DRAGONMAW GATES

THE WETLANDS

GRIM BATOL

ALGAZ GATE

MENETHIL HARBOR

IRONFORGE

STONEWROUGHT DAM

GNOMEREGAN

LOCH MODAN

KHARANOS

FARSTRIDER'S LODGE

DUN MOROGH

THELSAMAR

EXCAVATION SITE

COLDRIDGE VALLEY

STONEWROUGHT PASS

ULDAMAN

SEARING GORGE

LETHLOR RAVINE

THE CAULDRON

KARGATH

ANGOR FORTRESS

BLACKROCK MOUNTAIN

THE BADLANDS

DUSTBELCH GROTTO

BLACKROCK MOUNTAIN

FLAME CREST

RUINS OF THAURISSAN

BURNING STEPPES

STORMWIND

NORTHSIRE ABBEY

STONEWATCH KEEP

TOWER OF IL'GALAR

LAKESHIRE

EASTVALE CAMP

REDRIDGE MOUNTAINS

WESTRIDGE G

GOLDSHIRE

ELWYNN FOREST

FALLOW SANCTUARY

SWAMP OF SORROWS

TOWER OF AZORA

SUNKEN TEMPLE

DEADWIND PASS

WESTFALL

DUSKWOOD

STONARD

DARKSHIRE

SENTINEL HILL

RAVEN HILL

NETHERGARDE KEEP

KARAZHAN

MOONBROOK

BLASTED LANDS

THE DARK PORTAL

THE DEADMINES

ZUL'GURUB

THE TAINTED SCAR

ZUL'KUNDA

STRANGLETHORN VALE

THE VILE REEF

ZUL'MAMWE

GROM'GOL

THE ARENA

BOOTY BAY

Azeroth

I. History

A brief overview of the
Third War...and the founding
of the New Age.

Though the history of Azeroth is rife
with tales of war and unending struggle, the
invasion of the demonic Burning Legion stands
as the most destructive conflict ever known.

The Legion meticulously planned its return
to the mortal world over the course of
many long centuries.

Four years ago, their grand design came to
fruition at last.

The Scourge of Lordaeron

A generation past, the lords of the Burning Legion attempted to destroy the kingdoms of Azeroth by loosing the orcish Horde upon the world. Ultimately their plans were undone when the corrupt Horde buckled in upon itself due to incessant infighting. Undaunted, the demons surmised that a new and more unified force was necessary to sew chaos and disorder across the mortal world.

To this end, the demon Kil'jaeden created the Scourge – a vast army of undead warriors, united under the singular will of the dread Lich King. With the Lich King as his puppet, Kil'jaeden was able to rally the Scourge and prepare it to annihilate human civilization for all time. The Lich King and his mortal servant, Kel'Thuzad, planned to spread a terrible plague across the human lands, thereby swelling the ranks of the Scourge with newly risen undead warriors. Once their preparations were made, Kel'Thuzad and his Cult of the Damned struck the first blow against civilization by releasing the plague upon northern Lordaeron.

Uther the Lightbringer, one of humanity's most famous heroes, investigated the infected regions in the hope of finding a way to halt the plague's progress. Despite his efforts, the plague continued to spread and threatened to tear the Alliance apart. As the ranks of the undead swept across Lordaeron, the king's only son, Prince Arthas, took up the fight against the Scourge. Arthas succeeded in killing Kel'Thuzad, but even so, the Lich King's forces grew with every soldier that fell in battle. Frustrated and stymied by the seemingly unstoppable enemy, Arthas took increasingly extreme steps to hold back their advance. Finally Uther warned Arthas that he was losing his hold on humanity.

Arthas' fear and resolve proved to be his ultimate undoing. He tracked the plague's source to the arctic land of Northrend, intending to end its threat forever. Instead, he fell into the Lich King's trap when he took up the cursed runeblade Frostmourne in the belief that he could use it to save his people. The sword did indeed grant him unfathomable power; however, it also stole his soul. His spirit lost and his sanity shattered, Arthas was transformed into the greatest of the Lich King's death knights. He willingly led the Scourge against his own kingdom, slew Uther in battle, and murdered his own father, King Terenas. Caught off guard by Arthas' unthinkable crimes, Lordaeron was crushed under the Lich King's iron heel.

Sunwell – The Fall of Quel'Thalas

Though he had defeated all of the people he now saw as his enemies, Arthas was haunted by the ghost of Kel'Thuzad. The ghost told Arthas to bring Kel'Thuzad's remains to the mystical Sunwell, which was hidden within the high elves' kingdom of Quel'Thalas.

Accordingly, Arthas and his Scourge invaded Quel'Thalas and laid siege to the high elves' crumbling defenses. Sylvanas Windrunner, the Ranger-General of Silvermoon, put up a vallant fight, but Arthas eventually wiped out the high elf army and won through to the Sunwell. In a cruel gesture of his dominance, he even raised Sylvanas' defeated body as a banshee, cursed to mindless undeath in the service of Quel'Thalas' conqueror.

In due course, Arthas submerged Kel'Thuzad's remains within the holy waters of the Sunwell. Although the potent waters of Eternity were fouled by this act, Kel'Thuzad was reborn as a sorcerous lich. Resurrected as a far more powerful being, Kel'Thuzad explained the next phase of the Lich King's plan. By the time Arthas and his army of the dead turned southward, not one living elf remained in Quel'Thalas. The glorious homeland of the high elves, which had stood for more than nine thousand years, was no more.

Archimonde's Return and the Flight to Kalimdor

Once Kel'Thuzad was whole again, Arthas led the Scourge south towards Dalaran. There the lich would obtain the powerful spellbook of Medivh and use it to summon the demonlord Archimonde back into the world. From that point on, Archimonde himself would lead the Legion's final invasion. Not even the wizards of the Kirin Tor could stop Arthas' forces from stealing Medivh's book, and soon Kel'Thuzad had all he needed to perform the summoning. After ten thousand years, the mighty demon Archimonde and his host emerged once again upon the world of Azeroth. Yet Dalaran was not their final destination. Under orders from Kil'jaeden himself, Archimonde and his demons followed the undead Scourge to Kalimdor, bent on destroying Nordrassil, the World Tree.

In the midst of this chaos, a mysterious prophet appeared to lend the mortal races guidance. This prophet proved to be none other than Medivh, the last Guardian, miraculously returned from the Beyond to redeem himself for past sins. Medivh told the Horde and the Alliance of the dangers they faced and urged them to band together. Jaded by generations of hate, the orcs and humans would have none of it. Medivh was forced to deal with each race separately, using prophecy and trickery to guide them across the sea to the legendary land of Kalimdor. The orcs and humans soon encountered the long-hidden civilization of the night elves.

Led by their young warchief, Thrall, the orcs suffered a series of setbacks on their journey across Kalimdor's Barrens. Though they befriended Cairne Bloodhoof and his mighty tauren warriors, many orcs began to succumb to the demonic bloodlust that had plagued them for years. Even Thrall's greatest lieutenant, Grom Hellscream, betrayed the Horde by giving himself over to his baser instincts. As Hellscream and his loyal Warsong warriors stalked through the forests of Ashenvale, they clashed with the night elf Sentinels. Certain that the orcs had returned to their warlike ways, the demigod Cenarius came forth to drive Hellscream and his orcs back. Even so, Hellscream and his orcs, overcome with supernatural hate and rage, managed to kill Cenarius and corrupt the ancient forestlands. Hellscream later redeemed his honor, however, by helping Thrall defeat Mannoroth, the demonlord who first cursed the orcs with his bloodline of hate and rage. With Mannoroth's death, the orcs' blood-curse was finally brought to an end.

While Medivh worked to convince the orcs and humans of the need for an alliance, the night elves fought the Legion in their own secretive ways. Tyrande Whisperwind, the immortal High Priestess of the night elf Sentinels, battled desperately to keep the demons and undead from overrunning the forests of Ashenvale. Tyrande realized that she needed help, so she set out to awaken the night elf druids from their thousand-year slumber. Calling upon her love, Malfurion Stormrage, Tyrande succeeded in galvanizing her defenses and driving the Legion back. With Malfurion's help, nature herself rose up to vanquish the Legion and its Scourge allies.

While searching for more of the hibernating druids, Malfurion found the barrow prison in which he had chained his brother, Illidan. Convinced that Illidan would aid them against the Legion, Tyrande set him free. Though Illidan did aid them for a time, he eventually fled to pursue his own interests.

The night elves braced themselves and fought the Burning Legion with grim determination. The Legion had never ceased in its desire for the Well of Eternity, long the source of strength for the World Tree and itself the heart of the night elf kingdom. If their planned assault on the Tree was successful, the demons would literally tear the world apart.

The Battle of Mount Hyjal

Under Medivh's guidance, Thrall and Jaina Proudmoore – the leader of the human forces in Kalimdor – realized that they had to put aside their differences. Similarly, the night elves, led by Malfurion and Tyrande, agreed that they must unite if they hoped to defend the World Tree. Unified in purpose, the races of Azeroth worked together to fortify the World Tree's energies to their utmost. Empowered by the very strength of the world, Malfurion succeeded in unleashing Nordrassil's primal fury, utterly destroying Archimonde and severing the Legion's anchor to the Well of Eternity. The final battle shook the continent of Kalimdor to its roots. Unable to draw power from the Well itself, the Burning Legion crumbled under the combined might of the mortal armies.

The Betrayer Ascendant

During the Legion's invasion of Ashenvale, Tyrande released Illidan from his barrow prison, where he had spent ten thousand years of captivity. Initially he sought to appease his comrades, but soon he reverted to true form and consumed the energies of a powerful warlock artifact known as the Skull of Gul'dan. By doing so, Illidan developed demonic features and vastly magnified power. He also gained some of Gul'dan's old memories – especially those of the Tomb of Sargeras, the island dungeon rumored to hold the remains of the Dark Titan, Sargeras.

Bristling with power and free to roam the world once more, Illidan set out to find his own place in the scheme of things. However, Kil'jaeden confronted Illidan and made him an offer he could not refuse. Kil'jaeden was angered by Archimonde's defeat at Mount Hyjal, but he had bigger concerns than vengeance. Sensing that his creation, the Lich King, was growing too powerful to control, Kil'jaeden ordered Illidan to destroy Ner'zhul and put an end to the undead Scourge once and for all. In exchange, Illidan would receive untold power and a true place amongst the remaining lords of the Burning Legion.

Illidan agreed and immediately set out to destroy the Frozen Throne, the icy crystal cask in which the Lich King's spirit resided. Illidan knew that he would need a mighty artifact to destroy the Frozen Throne. Using the knowledge he had gained from Gul'dan's memories, Illidan decided to seek out the Tomb of Sargeras and claim the Dark Titan's remains. He called in some old Highborne debts and called the serpentine naga from their dark undersea lairs. Led by the cunning sea-witch, Lady Vashj, the naga helped Illidan reach the Broken Isles, where Sargeras' tomb was rumored to be located.

As Illidan set out with the naga, Warden Maiev Shadowsong began to hunt him. Maiev had been Illidan's jailor for ten thousand years and relished the prospect of recapturing him. Nevertheless, Illidan outsmarted Maiev and her Watchers and succeeded in claiming the Eye of Sargeras despite their efforts. With the powerful Eye in his possession, Illidan traveled to the former wizard-city of Dalaran. Strengthened by the city's ley power lines, Illidan used the Eye to cast a destructive spell against the Lich King's citadel of Icecrown in distant Northrend. Illidan's attack shattered the Lich King's defenses and ruptured the very roof of the world. At the final moment, Illidan's destructive spell was stopped when his brother Malfurion and the Priestess Tyrande arrived to aid Maiev.

Knowing that Kil'jaeden would not be pleased with his failure to destroy the Frozen Throne, Illidan fled to the barren dimension known as Outland: the last remnants of Draenor, the orcs' former homeworld. There he intended to plan his next moves while evading Kil'jaeden's wrath. After they succeeded in stopping Illidan, Tyrande and Malfurion returned home to Ashenvale Forest to watch over their people. Maiev, however, would not quit so easily, and followed Illidan to Outland, determined to bring him to justice.

Rise of the Blood Elves

At this time, the undead Scourge had essentially transformed Lordaeron and Quel'Thalas into the toxic Plaguelands. There were only a few pockets of Alliance resistance forces left. One such group, consisting primarily of high elves, was led by the last of the Sunstrider dynasty: Prince Kael'thas. Kael, an accomplished wizard himself, grew wary of the failing Alliance, which treated its elven allies with suspicion and hostility. The high elves grieved for the loss of their homeland and decided to call themselves blood elves in honor of their fallen people. Yet as they worked to keep the Scourge at bay, they suffered considerably at being cut off from the Sunwell that had empowered them. When the Alliance ordered the blood elves to fight against nearly impossible odds, the naga offered assistance that turned the tide of battle. Unfortunately the Alliance learned of Kael's association with the naga and condemned him and his people as traitors. Imprisoned and condemned to death, the blood elves were rescued by Lady Vashj.

With no other place left to go, Kael and his blood elves followed Lady Vashj to Outland. Together they sought out Warden Maiev Shadowsong, who had recaptured Illidan. It was only a matter of time until the combined naga and blood elf forces managed to defeat her and free Illidan from her grasp. According to Illidan, there was no cure for the blood elves' racial addiction to magic. Illidan had a different proposal in mind: in return for the blood elves' loyalty, he would grant them all the magic they could desire. It was an offer Kael had to accept: he was certain his people would die without either a cure or a new source of magic. Kael embraced his people's Highborne ancestry and joined the naga. Based in Outland, Illidan gathered his redoubled forces for a second strike against the Lich King and his fortress of Icecrown.

Civil War in the Plaguelands

Ner'zhul, the Lich King, knew that his time was short. Imprisoned within the Frozen Throne, he suspected that Kil'jaeden would send his agents to destroy him. The damage caused by Illidan's spell had ruptured the Frozen Throne, and the Lich King was losing his power daily. Desperate to save himself, he called out to his greatest mortal servant: the death knight who now called himself King Arthas.

Meanwhile, Arthas had become embroiled in a civil war in Lordaeron. Half of the standing undead forces, led by the banshee Sylvanas Windrunner, staged a coup for control over the undead empire. As the Lich King's strength waned, so too did Arthas' powers. Alerted to the Lich King's peril, Arthas struck out for the north and left the Scourge in the hands of his lieutenant, Kel'Thuzad, as the war escalated throughout the Plaguelands.

Ultimately Sylvanas and her rebel undead (known as the Forsaken) claimed the ruined capital city of Lordaeron as their own. Constructing their own bastion, far beneath the wrecked city, the Forsaken vowed to defeat the Scourge and drive Kel'Thuzad and his minions from the land.

Weakened, but determined to save his master, Arthas reached Northrend only to find Illidan's naga and blood elves waiting for him. Arthas and his nerubian allies raced against Illidan's forces to reach the Icecrown Glacier and defend the Frozen Throne.

The Lich King Triumphant

Even weakened as he was, Arthas outmaneuvered Illidan and reached the Frozen Throne first. Using his runeblade, Frostmourne, Arthas shattered the Lich King's icy prison and thereby released Ner'zhul's enchanted helm and breastplate. Arthas placed the unimaginably powerful helm on his head, and Ner'zhul and Arthas' spirits fused into a single mighty being, as Ner'zhul had planned all along. Illidan and his troops were forced to flee back to Outland in disgrace, and Arthas became one of the most powerful entities the world has ever known.

Currently Arthas, the new and immortal Lich King, resides in Northrend; he is rumored to be rebuilding the citadel of Icecrown. His trusted lieutenant, Kel'Thuzad, commands the Scourge in the Plaguelands. Sylvanas and her rebel Forsaken hold only the Tirisfal Glades, a small portion of the war-torn kingdom.

Old Hatreds –
The Colonization of Kalimdor

Though victory was theirs, the mortal races found themselves in a world shattered by war. The Scourge and the Burning Legion had all but destroyed Lordaeron, and had almost finished the job in Kalimdor. There were forests to heal, grudges to bury, and home-lands to settle. The war had wounded each race deeply, but they had selflessly banded together to attempt a new beginning, starting with the uneasy truce between the Alliance and Horde.

Thrall led the orcs to the continent of Kalimdor, where they founded a new homeland with the help of their tauren brethren. Naming their new land Durotar after Thrall's murdered father, the orcs settled down to rebuild their once-glorious society. Now that the demon curse was ended, the Horde changed from a warlike juggernaut into more of a loose coalition, dedicated to survival and prosperity rather than conquest. Aided by the noble tauren and the cunning trolls of the Darkspear tribe, Thrall and his orcs looked forward to a new era of peace in their own land.

The remaining Alliance forces under Jaina Proudmoore settled in southern Kalimdor. Off the eastern coast of Dustwallow Marsh, they built the rugged port city of Theramore. There, the humans and their dwarven allies worked to survive in a land that would always be hostile to them. Though the defenders of Durotar and Theramore kept the tentative truce with one another, the fragile colonial serenity was not meant to last.

The peace between the orcs and humans was shattered by the arrival of a massive Alliance fleet in Kalimdor. The mighty fleet, under the command of Grand Admiral Daelin Proudmoore (Jaina's father), had left Lordaeron before Arthas destroyed the kingdom. Having sailed for many grueling months, Admiral Proudmoore was searching for any Alliance survivors he could find.

Proudmoore's armada posed a serious threat to the stability of the region. As a renowned hero of the Second War, Jaina's father was a staunch enemy of the Horde, and he was determined to destroy Durotar before the orcs could gain a foothold in the land.

The Grand Admiral forced Jaina to make a terrible decision: support him in battle against the orcs and betray her newfound allies, or fight her own father to maintain the fragile peace that the Alliance and the Horde had finally attained. After much soul-searching, Jaina chose the latter and helped Thrall defeat her crazed father. Unfortunately Admiral Proudmoore died in battle before Jaina could reconcile with him or prove that orcs were no longer bloodthirsty monsters. For her loyalty, the orcs allowed Jaina's forces to return home safely to Theramore.

II. Races in Conflict

HUMANS

The noble humans of Stormwind are a proud, tenacious race. They bravely fought the orcish Horde for generations as the patrons of the Grand Alliance. Just as they thought peace had at last settled over their war-torn kingdoms, an even darker shadow descended upon the world. The undead Scourge unleashed a foul plague of death upon humanity and succeeded in decimating the northern human kingdom of Lordaeron. The few humans who survived fled south to the protection of Stormwind. Yet no sooner had the undead struck than the demonic Burning Legion began its cataclysmic invasion of the world. The warriors of humanity stood fast against the Legion and helped save the world from imminent destruction.

Nearly four years later, the defenders of Stormwind stand vigilant against any who would threaten the sanctity of their lands. Situated in the foothills of Elwynn Forest, Stormwind City is one of the last bastions of human power in the world. The child-king Anduin Wrynn rules the people of Stormwind, who remain steadfast in their commitment to the Grand Alliance. Backed by their stalwart allies, the armies of Stormwind have been called away to once again fight the savage Horde on distant battlefields. With the armies gone, the defense of Stormwind now falls to its proud citizens.

You must defend the kingdom against those who encroach upon it, and hunt down the subversive traitors who seek to destroy it from within. Now is the time for heroes. Now humanity's greatest chapter can be told.

STORMWIND

The city of Stormwind stands as the last bastion of human power in Azeroth. Rebuilt after the Second War, Stormwind is a marvel of human design and engineering. Stormwind's guards keep the peace within the city's walls, and its young king, Anduin Wrynn, rules from his mighty keep. The Trade District bustles with trade from across the continent and beyond, while adventurers of every sort can be found wandering the streets of Old Town. Unaffected by the ravages of the Scourge in the north, Stormwind still faces its own threats, both from without and from within.

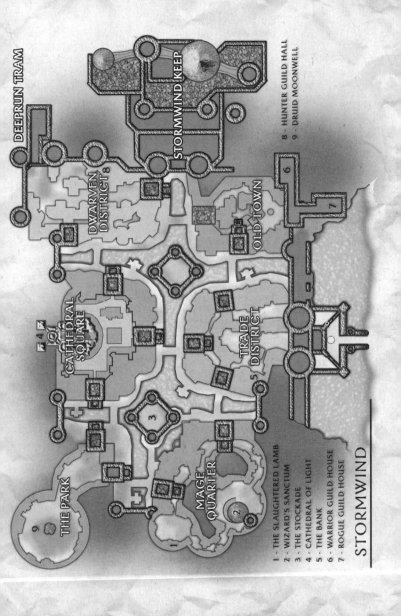

DEEPRUN TRAM

STORMWIND KEEP

DWARVEN DISTRICT 8

CATHEDRAL SQUARE

THE PARK

MAGE QUARTER

TRADE DISTRICT

OLD TOWN

1 - THE SLAUGHTERED LAMB
2 - WIZARD'S SANCTUM
3 - THE STOCKADE
4 - CATHEDRAL OF LIGHT
5 - THE BANK
6 - WARRIOR GUILD HOUSE
7 - ROGUE GUILD HOUSE
8 - HUNTER GUILD HALL
9 - DRUID MOONWELL

STORMWIND

NOTABLE HUMANS

King Anduin Wrynn - King Anduin is as wise a ruler as any ten-year-old has a right to be. Recently his father, King Varian Wrynn, went missing under suspicious circumstances while en route to a diplomatic summit at Theramore Isle. At the behest of the royal councilor, Lady Prestor, young Anduin was given the crown so that order could be preserved within the kingdom of Stormwind. Though few citizens are aware that their true king has been missing for so long, Anduin does the best he can to allay their fears. It is widely held that the boy will grow to become a shrewd leader one day.

Archbishop Benedictus - In his youth, the kindly Benedictus was the student of Lordaeron's religious leader, Archbishop Alonsus Faol. Benedictus spent many years learning from his pious master and helped the Church of Light construct its most striking monument, the Cathedral in Stormwind. Following the Faol's death, Benedictus took charge of the Church and swore to continue the good work his mentor had begun so many years ago.

Jaina Proudmoore - Jaina Proudmoore is the most powerful human sorceress alive. A one-time ally of Prince Arthas, Jaina saw the fall of Lordaeron firsthand. Traveling to Kalimdor, Jaina swore to defeat the Burning Legion and its sinister agents any way she could. Joining forces with the night elves and even the orcish Horde, Jaina helped defeat the demon Archimonde and banish the Legion forever. She then gathered the human survivors in Kalimdor and founded the port city of Theramore. There she rules over the tattered remnants of the Alliance and hopes to reunite the distant human kingdoms once more.

DWARVES

The stoic dwarves of Ironforge spent countless generations mining treasures from deep within the earth. Secure in their impregnable stronghold of Ironforge Mountain, the dwarves rarely ventured beyond the wintry peaks of Dun Morogh. Even so, when the orcs invaded Azeroth and set out to conquer the human, elven, and dwarven lands, the dwarves offered to join the Grand Alliance. The resilient and ingenious dwarves proved to be the backbone of the Alliance forces and helped usher in victory after victory.

Recently the dwarves unearthed a series of ruins that held the key to the secrets of their lost heritage. Driven to discover the truth about his people's fabled origins, King Magni Bronzebeard ordered that the dwarves shift their industry from mining and engineering to that of archaeology. Magni helped to create the famed Explorers' Guild of Ironforge, a group utterly devoted to plumbing the secrets of the ancient world and delving out the truth of the dwarves' fabled existence.

An integral part of the Grand Alliance, the rugged dwarven armies have been called away to battle the merciless Horde in faraway lands. In these perilous times, the defense of the mountain kingdom falls to brave dwarves like you. The spirits of the dwarven kings watch over you, and the very mountains are your strength. The future of your people is in your hands.

IRONFORGE

Many dwarven strongholds fell during the Second War, but the mighty city of Ironforge, nestled in the wintry peaks of Dun Morogh, was never breached by the invading Horde. A marvel to the dwarves' skill at shaping rock and stone, Ironforge was constructed in the heart of the mountain itself: an expansive underground city of explorers, miners, and warriors. While the Alliance has been weakened by recent events, the dwarves of Ironforge, led by King Magni Bronzebeard, are forging a new future in the world.

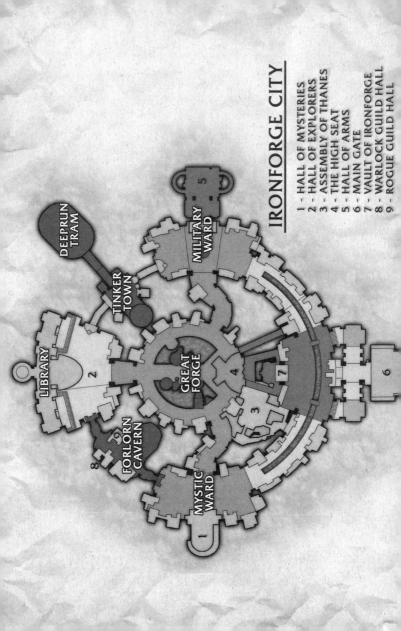

IRONFORGE CITY

1 - HALL OF MYSTERIES
2 - HALL OF EXPLORERS
3 - ASSEMBLY OF THANES
4 - THE HIGH SEAT
5 - HALL OF ARMS
6 - MAIN GATE
7 - VAULT OF IRONFORGE
8 - WARLOCK GUILD HALL
9 - ROGUE GUILD HALL

DEEPRUN TRAM

LIBRARY

TINKER TOWN

GREAT FORGE

FORLORN CAVERN

MILITARY WARD

MYSTIC WARD

NOTABLE DWARVES

King Magni Bronzebeard - The eldest of the three Bronzebeard brothers, Magni was destined to be the king under the mountain. Strong of arm and keen of mind, Magni loved his two brothers above all else in the world. During the recent fall of Lordaeron, his middle brother, Muradin, was killed by the death knight Prince Arthas. Magni was overcome with grief at the news of Muradin's demise, but he and the youngest brother, Brann, remained steadfast in their desire to continue serving the dwarven people. Brann, an explorer of some renown, went missing only months ago, and King Magni has lost hope that Brann still lives. Though he remains a wise and strong leader, his pain and sorrow weigh heavily upon him. Many dwarves wonder whether the kingdom will ever see another Bronzebeard sitting on the High Throne of Ironforge.

Brann Bronzebeard - One of the greatest explorers to ever wander the lands of Azeroth, Brann Bronzebeard was recognized and welcomed across the known world. The warm, courageous dwarf had made friends and acquaintances in nearly every charted land – and presumably those uncharted as well. Brann spent many years mapping out the remote corners and hidden nooks of the Eastern Kingdoms for his beloved Explorers' Guild. With the recent discovery of Kalimdor, Brann was one of the first dwarves to tread the unknown paths of the ancients. Little is known about Brann's recent disappearance other than the fact that he was headed towards the continent of Northrend to investigate his brother Muradin's death. It is unknown whether or not he ever made it to the icy shores of that land.

High Explorer Magellas - Muninn Magellas has had an insatiable curiosity for history and arcana since he was a small boy. Now, as the patron of the Explorers' Guild, his childhood wish has come true. Magellas is responsible for mapping out the world and cataloguing its various species, relics, and treasures for the generations to come. Employing a small army of Prospectors, Magellas has sent his agents all over the world to gain knowledge and insight for his people. Like King Magni, Magellas was grieved to hear of Brann's loss. Nevertheless, he is committed to steering the Explorers' Guild and gaining valuable insight on the mistakes of the past.

GNOMES

The eccentric, often brilliant gnomes are held as one of the most peculiar races of the world. With their obsession for developing radical new technologies and constructing marvels of mind-bending engineering, it's a wonder that any gnomes have survived to proliferate. Over the years, the gnomes have contributed ingenious weapons to aid the Grand Alliance in its fierce battles against the Horde.

Thriving in the wondrous techno-city of Gnomeregan, the gnomes shared the resources of the forested peaks of Dun Morogh with their dwarven cousins for generations. Yet recently, a barbaric menace rose up from the bowels of the earth and invaded Gnomeregan. The troggs – believed to have been unearthed from the Uldaman excavation – erupted beneath Gnomeregan and began to slaughter every gnome within the city. Though the gnomish defense forces staged a valiant defense, they could not save their wondrous city.

At the command of the High Tinker Mekkatorque, the gnomes opened the pressure valves of their giant, grinding machines and released toxic radiation throughout the city. Though the radiation killed the troggs, the gnomes soon discovered that it killed their own people just as quickly. Nearly eighty percent of the gnomish race died within days. Those that survived evacuated the great city and fled to the protection of their dwarven cousins in Ironforge.

There they remain, devising radical strategies to retake their beloved city at any cost. As a gnome of proud standing, it falls to you to answer the challenge and lead your curious people to a brighter future.

NOTABLE GNOMES

High Tinker Mekkatorque - The gnomes have not had a proper king or queen for over four hundred years. Instead, they prefer to elect their highest officials for set terms of service. The highest office in Gnomeregan, High Tinker, has been held by the crafty Gelbin Mekkatorque for the past seven years. Gelbin is one of the most renowned inventors ever, and has been honored as a just and skillful leader. However, when the troggs began their invasion of Gnomeregan, Gelbin was unprepared to stop them. At the behest of his top advisor, Mekgineer Thermaplugg, he ordered that the city be bathed in toxic radiation. Though the radiation stopped the raiders' advance, it ultimately killed more gnomes than troggs. Now the High Tinker carries the weight of the dead on his shoulders and seeks to avenge his people by reclaiming their lost city.

Mekgineer Thermaplugg - Sicco Thermaplugg served as High Tinker Mekkatorque's chief advisor for many years. A brooding but imaginative engineer, Thermaplugg secretly coveted the role of High Tinker. It is rumored that Thermaplugg actually knew of the trogg invasion before it began, and that he ushered in the events that befell the gnomish race. Though these reports were never verified, Mekkatorque believes they could be true. Mekgineer Thermaplugg disappeared shortly after the evacuation of the irradiated city. None can say whether or not he still lives within the toxic halls of Gnomeregan.

NIGHT ELVES

For ten thousand years, the immortal night elves cultivated a druidic society within the shadowed recesses of Ashenvale Forest. Then the catastrophic invasion of the Burning Legion shattered the tranquility of their ancient civilization. Led by the Arch-Druid Malfurion Stormrage and the Priestess Tyrande Whisperwind, the mighty night elves rose to challenge the demonic onslaught. Aided by the newly arrived orcs and humans, the night elves succeeded in halting the Legion's advance and defeating its master, the demonlord Archimonde. Though victorious, the night elves were forced to sacrifice their cherished immortality and watch their beloved forests burn.

In the aftermath of the horrific conflict, Malfurion and Tyrande helped their people rebuild their shattered villages. Slowly the night elves began to adjust to their mortal existence. Such an adjustment was far from easy, and there were many night elves who could not adjust to the prospects of aging, disease, and frailty. Seeking to regain their immortality, a number of wayward druids conspired to plant a special tree that would reestablish link between their spirits and the eternal world. When Malfurion heard about this plan, he warned that nature would never bless such a selfish act. Shortly thereafter, Malfurion's spirit was somehow lost within the depths of the Emerald Dream. Though his fellow druids attempted to find his wandering spirit, only his body remained sleeping within his Barrow Den.

With Malfurion missing, Fandral Staghelm – the leader of those who wished to plant the new World Tree – became the new Arch-Druid. In no time at all, he and his fellow druids had forged ahead and planted the great tree, Teldrassil, off the stormy coasts of northern Kalimdor. Under their care, the tree sprouted up above the clouds. Among the twilight boughs of the colossal tree, the wondrous city of Darnassus took root. However, the tree was not consecrated with nature's blessing and soon fell prey to the corruption of the Burning Legion. Now the wildlife and even the limbs of Teldrassil itself are tainted by a growing darkness.

As one of the few night elves still left in the world, it is your sworn duty to defend Darnassus and the wild children of nature against the Legion's encroaching corruption.

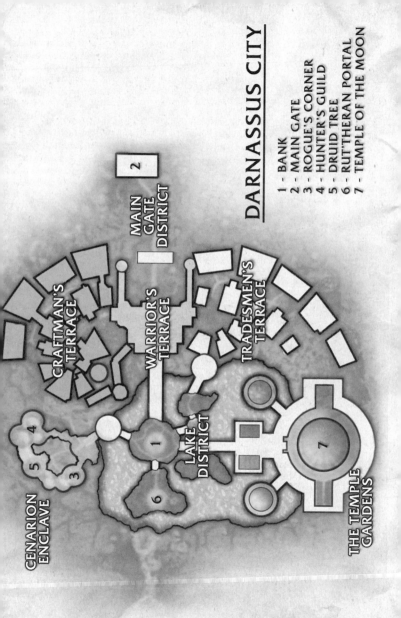

DARNASSUS CITY

1 - BANK
2 - MAIN GATE
3 - ROGUE'S CORNER
4 - HUNTER'S GUILD
5 - DRUID TREE
6 - RUT'THERAN PORTAL
7 - TEMPLE OF THE MOON

CENARION ENCLAVE

CRAFTMAN'S TERRACE

MAIN GATE DISTRICT

WARRIOR'S TERRACE

TRADESMEN'S TERRACE

LAKE DISTRICT

THE TEMPLE GARDENS

DARNASSUS CITY

High atop the boughs of the enormous tree Teldrassil is the won drous city of Darnassus, the new refuge of the reclusive nigh elves. Druids, hunters, and warriors alike make their homes among the rows of wood-crafted lodges and delicately tended groves. The Temple of the Moon rises like a shining beacon above the trees flanked by the colonnaded Hall of Justice, where the vigilan Sentinels gather to safeguard the land. Ruled by the High Priestes Tyrande Whisperwind, Darnassus stands as a tranquil testament to all that the night elves hold sacred. A city in tune with the rush and flow of nature, Darnassus was built along the shores of a large lake with elegant bridges spanning its crystalline waters. Elsewhere, the falling leaves of the forest carpet the soft pathways of the city.

NOTABLE NIGHT ELVES

Tyrande Whisperwind - Tyrande is the High Priestess of the moon goddess, Elune. She has served as the leader of the nigh elf Sentinels for nearly ten thousand years, but her long vigil ha left her with little mercy for those she regards as her foe. A exceptional and fearless warrior, she stands as one of the greates heroes in recorded history. Following the catastrophic invasion o the Burning Legion, Tyrande ruled over her people alongside he mate, the Arch-Druid Malfurion Stormrage, until he disappeare into the mystic Emerald Dream. With Malfurion inexplicably los Tyrande has again become the sole ruler of her prideful people Troubled by Malfurion's disappearance, she nevertheless strives t keep the night elves from reliving the mistakes of the past.

Malfurion Stormrage - The greatest druid ever to live, and arguably on of the most powerful beings in history, Malfurion Stormrage stands a both prophet and savior to his people. Under the leadership of Tyrand and Malfurion, the night elves vanquished the Burning Legion no once, but twice. To replenish his powers, Malfurion periodically hibe nates within the spirit realm known as the Emerald Dream. Recentl something went wrong with Malfurion's dreamstate. Now he is trappe somewhere within the dream, beyond even the reach of the gree dragons whose realm it is. With Malfurion lost, the night elves w certainly stumble into darkness, just as they have since time immemoria

Fandral Staghelm - One of Malfurion's top lieutenants, Fandral is clever druid who has trained many of the newest generation of druid of the wild. His hot temperament has sometimes clashed with th more restrained Malfurion. Fandral believes that the future of the nigh elves demands more expansionism and military planning. His radic beliefs and aggressive demeanor often lead him to quarrel open with the High Priestess, Tyrande. Regardless, to this date, Fandral ha proven to be an effective replacement for the missing Malfurion.

ORCS

Long ago, the noble orcish race was corrupted by the Burning Legion and transformed into the merciless, destructive Horde. Lured to the world of Azeroth, the orcs were forced to make war upon the human kingdoms of Stormwind and Lordaeron. Though the Horde nearly succeeded in annihilating humanity, it ultimately devoured itself from within and collapsed. The defeated orcs spent many years within guarded prisons, unable to function without the prospect of conquest and warfare. After many years, a visionary young warchief rose to lead his people in their darkest hour. Fittingly enough, the young orc's name was Thrall. Under his rule, the orcs freed themselves from the chains of demonic corruption and embraced their shamanistic heritage.

At the behest of a strange prophet, Thrall led his people to the ancient lands of Kalimdor. There, Thrall and the Horde came face to face with their old oppressor, the Burning Legion. With the aid of the humans and night elves, the orcs defeated the Legion and set out to find their own path in their adopted world. The orcs claimed the harsh wastelands of Durotar as their kingdom in Kalimdor.

Now based in the warrior city of Orgrimmar, the orcs look forward to a shining new future for their people. Though they are no longer driven by dreams of conquest, they stand ready to destroy all who would challenge their sovereignty or their supremacy. It is your duty to crush the enemies of Durotar, both seen and unseen, for the nefarious agents of the Burning Legion still wander the land.

ORGRIMMAR

Named in honor of the legendary Orgrim Doomhammer, Orgrimmar was founded as the capital city of the orcs' new home land. Built within a huge, winding canyon in the harsh land of Durotar, Orgrimmar stands as one of the mightiest warrior cities in the world. Behind Orgrimmar's immense walls, elderly shaman pass their knowledge on to the Horde's newest generation of leaders, while warriors spar in the gladiatorial arena, honing their skill in preparation for the trials that await them in this dangerous land.

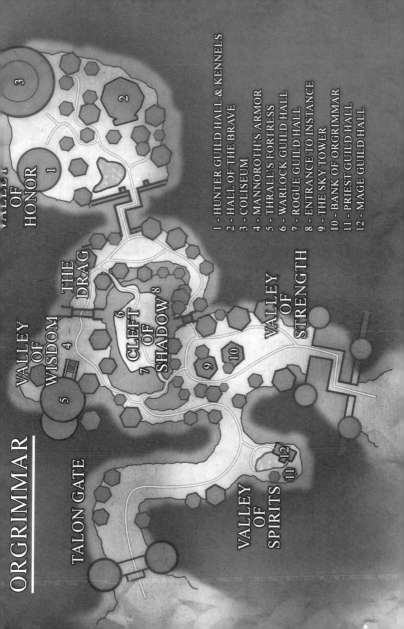

ORGRIMMAR

TALON GATE

VALLEY OF HONOR

VALLEY OF WISDOM

THE DRAG

CLEFT OF SHADOW

VALLEY OF STRENGTH

VALLEY OF SPIRITS

1 - HUNTER GUILD HALL & KENNELS
2 - HALL OF THE BRAVE
3 - COLISEUM
4 - MANNOROTH'S ARMOR
5 - THRALL'S FORTRESS
6 - WARLOCK GUILD HALL
7 - ROGUE GUILD HALL
8 - ENTRANCE TO INSTANCE
9 - THE SKY TOWER
10 - BANK OF ORGRIMMAR
11 - PRIEST GUILD HALL
12 - MAGE GUILD HALL

NOTABLE ORCS

Thrall - Thrall, the son of Durotan, is perhaps the mightiest orc alive. Armed with the mighty Doomhammer, Thrall is a peerless warrior and powerful shaman. He stands as warchief over the entire Horde, holding dominion over the Darkspear trolls and tauren tribes alike. His honor, cunning, and compassion have won him many allies over the years, even amongst the humans and night elves. Thrall lives to defend his people's freedom and ensure the safety of the extended Horde.

Nazgrel - Nazgrel was the preeminent warrior of the Frostwolf clan, which had once been ruled by Thrall's father. When Thrall joined the clan, Nazgrel was initially unwilling to accept him, but after Thrall had proven himself in battle, Nazgrel learned to respect the younger orc. Since then, Nazgrel has served as Thrall's general and chief of security. It is Nazgrel's duty to protect Durotar from internal threats and anarchy. He is a grim and fearsome orc utterly committed to his warchief and the glory of the Horde.

Drek'Thar - The elder shaman of the Frostwolf clan, Drek'Thar served as Thrall's tutor many years ago. Blind since birth, Drek'Thar had to prove his worth during the Horde's dark period. He found the spirits of the elements to be close companions, so shamanism became his path to might. Despite his power over the elements, Drek'Thar has always maintained his meekness and wisdom. He continues to shepherd the younger shaman of the Horde in the old traditions of his people.

TAUREN

For countless generations, the bestial tauren roamed the plains of the Barrens, hunted the mighty kodos, and sought the wisdom of their eternal goddess, the Earth Mother. Scattered across the land, the wandering tribes were united only by a common hatred for their sworn enemy, the marauding centaur. Seeking aid against the centaur, the chieftain, Cairne Bloodhoof, befriended Warchief Thrall and the other orcs, who had recently journeyed to Kalimdor.

With the orcs' help, Cairne and his Bloodhoof tribe were able to drive back the centaur and claim the grasslands of Mulgore for their own. For the first time in hundreds of years, the tauren had a land to call their own. Upon the windswept mesa of Thunder Bluff, Cairne built a refuge for his people, where tauren of every tribe is welcome. Over time, the scattered tauren tribes united under Cairne's rule. There are a few tribes who disagree about the direction their new nation should take, but all agree that Cairne is the wisest and best suited to lead them towards the future.

Though the noble tauren are peaceful in nature, the rites of the Great Hunt are venerated as the heart of their spiritual culture. Every tauren, warrior or otherwise, seeks identity both as a hunter and as a child of the Earth Mother. Having reached the age of maturity, you must test your skills in the wild and prove yourself in the Great Hunt.

THUNDER BLUFF

The city of Thunder Bluff lies atop a series of mesas that overlook the verdant grasslands of Mulgore. Once a nomadic people, the tauren recently established the city as a center for trade caravans, traveling artisans, and inventors of every kind. The proud city also stands as a refuge for the many hunters who stalk their dangerous prey through the Barrens and its surrounding areas. Long bridges of wood and rope span the chasms between the mesas, and each mesa is topped with tents, longhouses, colorfully painted totems, and spirit lodges. The mighty chief, Cairne Bloodhoof, presides over the bustling city, ensuring that the united tauren tribes live in peace and security.

THUNDER BLUFF

1 - SHAMAN GUILD HALL
2 - POOLS OF VISION
3 - DRUID GUILD HALL
4 - HUNTER & WARRIOR
    GUILD HALL
5 - CHIEFTAIN'S TENT
6 - BANK OF THUNDER BLUFF

ELDER RISE

SPIRIT RISE

HUNTER RISE

NOTABLE TAUREN

Cairne Bloodhoof - Cairne is dedicated to serving his people and to watching over their safety in an ever-darkening world. An outstanding warrior, Cairne is considered one of the most dangerous creatures alive. Despite his strength and valor, he is a gentle soul who longs only for the peace and tranquility of the open plains. It is rumored that if he could lay the responsibilities of chieftain on another, Cairne would leave Thunder Bluff in an instant and retire to the wilds. Many believe that he is training his son, Baine, to take his place as chieftain one fateful day.

Magatha Grimtotem - Magatha is the elder crone of the mighty Grimtotem clan. Blessed with shamanic powers when she was just a young girl, Magatha has sought power and prestige nearly her whole life. She became the matriarch of the Grimtotem clan through an arranged marriage that many suspect she arranged herself, but subsequently lost her mate to an unforeseen climbing accident. Since her mate's death, Magatha has commanded the stern Grimtotem warriors. The Grimtotems believe that Magatha will lead them in eradicating the lesser races from Kalimdor and retaking the tauren's ancestral holdings abroad. Magatha constantly spars with Cairne Bloodhoof over the direction of the tauren's future and feels that only she is fit to rule her people.

Hamuul Runetotem - A childhood friend of Cairne Bloodhoof, Hamuul Runetotem serves as the elder druid of Thunder Bluff. Hamuul befriended the mighty night elf Malfurion Stormrage during the recent invasion of the Burning Legion. The great druid taught Hamuul many secrets of the wild and blessed him with the touch of nature. Since that time, Hamuul has become an honored member of the (predominantly night elf) Cenarion Circle, and is recognized as the first tauren druid in nearly twenty generations. Hamuul is a fierce supporter of Cairne Bloodhoof and teaches the ways of druidism to his honored brethren.

TROLLS

The vicious trolls that populate the numerous jungle isles of the South Seas are renowned for their cruelty and dark mysticism. Barbarous and superstitious, they carry a seething hatred for all other races. At the height of the Gurubashi Empire, the jungle trolls ruled over the lands from Stranglethorn Vale in Azeroth to the Echo Isles of Kalimdor. However, at the apex of their reign, the Gurubashi people splintered into a handful of warring tribes. One such tribe, the Darkspear tribe, was driven from its lands and forced to fend for itself amidst the deadly jungle races of Stranglethorn.

After generations of loss and servitude to larger and less honorable tribes, the Darkspears faced possible extinction. Though their warriors were amongst the bravest ever born, the incessant politics of the Gurubashi tribes threatened to end the Darkspears' way of life. Even worse, humans began erecting settlements in Stranglethorn as well. It was during this dire time that the Darkspears met Warchief Thrall and the warriors of the orcish Horde.

The Darkspears, led by the aged witch doctor, Sen'jin, appealed to Thrall and his Horde for help against the human invaders. Together the trolls and orcs won the day, but it proved to be a short-lived victory. The local murlocs captured many of the victors and prepared to sacrifice them to a sea witch. The Darkspears fought alongside the Horde, but the noble Sen'jin fell during the final battle against the murlocs.

In honor of Sen'jin's sacrifice, Thrall vowed that the Darkspears would always have a place within the Horde. He offered the trolls sanctuary in the new kingdom he and his orcs planned to build across the sea. Vol'jin, the son of Sen'jin, took control of the Darkspear tribe and wished Thrall farewell. Nearly one year later he finally led his people to Kalimdor and made a home for them on the Echo Isles, just off the rugged crimson coastline of Durotar. As one of the only surviving Darkspears, it falls to you to reclaim the glory of your tribe.

Though the Darkspears originally settled in the Echo Isles, they were betrayed by one of their own, a crazed sorcerer named Zalazane. Forced to flee from their island holdings, the Darkspears created the fishing village of Sen'jin on the Durotar coast. From this crude village, the Darkspears and their allies strike at Zalazane's holdings on the Echo Isles, determined to win back their jungle home at any cost.

NOTABLE TROLLS

Vol'jin - Vol'jin is a powerful shadow hunter and one of the most cunning trolls alive. His father, Sen'jin, fell in battle while aiding Thrall and the Horde, and Vol'jin has sworn to use all of his powers and wisdom to lead his tribe just as his father would have. Vol'jin's crafty stratagems and quick wit have served Thrall well over the years. He spends most of his time in the orcs' city of Orgrimmar, consulting with Thrall and helping to expand the Horde's security and influence over Kalimdor.

Master Gadrin - Gadrin is one of Vol'jin's most trusted advisers. Along with a young witch doctor named Zalazane, Gadrin led the mystical training of many Darkspear priests and mages. However, Zalazane went mad from the mystical forces he had unleashed. The crazed witch doctor placed a curse upon the Echo Isles and drove Gadrin and his brethren away.

Now Gadrin seeks to end Zalazane's rampage and put the souls of his cursed brethren to rest.

UNDEAD (FORSAKEN)

Bound to the iron will of the tyrant Lich King, the vast undead armies of the Scourge seek to eradicate all life on Azeroth. Led by the banshee Sylvanas Windrunner, one group of undead broke away from the Scourge and freed themselves of the Lich King's domination. These renegades call themselves the Forsaken. They fight a constant battle not only to retain their freedom from the Scourge, but also to exterminate those who would hunt them as monsters.

With Sylvanas as their banshee queen, the Forsaken have built a dark stronghold beneath the ruins of Lordaeron's former capital city. This hidden 'Undercity' forms a sprawling labyrinth that stretches beneath the haunted woods of the Tirisfal Glades. From this bastion, the Forsaken wage an unending battle against the Scourge as well as the remaining humans who still seek to reclaim their lands. For though the very land is cursed, the zealous humans of the Scarlet Crusade cling to their scattered holdings, obsessed with eradicating the undead and retaking their once-beautiful homeland.

Convinced that the primitive races of the Horde can help them achieve victory over their enemies, the Forsaken have entered an alliance of convenience with the savage orcs and the proud tauren. Harboring no true loyalty for their new allies, they will go to any lengths to ensure their dark plans come to fruition.

As one of the Forsaken, you must eliminate any who pose a threat to the new order — be they human, undead, or otherwise.

UNDERCITY

Far beneath the ruined capital city of Lordaeron, the royal crypts have been turned into a bastion of evil and undeath. Arthas originally intended the Undercity to be the Scourge's seat of power, but the budding city was abandoned when he was recalled to aid the Lich King in distant Northrend. In Arthas' absence, the Dark Lady, Sylvanas Windrunner, led the rebel Forsaken to the Undercity and claimed it for her own. Since taking up residence the Forsaken have worked to complete the Undercity's construction by dredging out the twisted maze of catacombs, tombs, and dungeons that Arthas began.

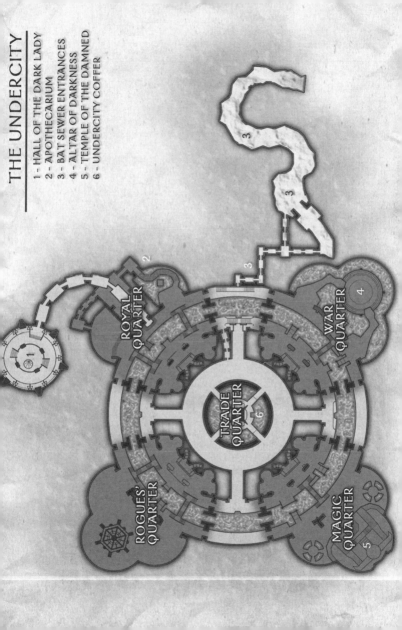

THE UNDERCITY

1 - HALL OF THE DARK LADY
2 - APOTHECARIUM
3 - BAT SEWER ENTRANCES
4 - ALTAR OF DARKNESS
5 - TEMPLE OF THE DAMNED
6 - UNDERCITY COFFER

ROYAL QUARTER

WAR QUARTER

TRADE QUARTER

ROGUES' QUARTER

MAGIC QUARTER

NOTABLE FORSAKEN

Sylvanas Windrunner - Before the coming of the plague, Sylvanas Windrunner was the brave Ranger-General of Silvermoon. During the Third War, Prince Arthas invaded the elven kingdom of Quel'Thalas. Sylvanas led her forces in a desperate struggle against the undead Scourge, but Arthas eventually defeated the high elves and transformed Sylvanas into one of his banshee slaves. Cursed to mindless undeath, Sylvanas only regained her will when the Lich King's powers waned. Eventually she outwitted the Scourge and broke away with her rebel faction, which she came to be known as the Forsaken. Now she rules over the Forsaken from the Undercity of Lordaeron. Her goal is to take vengeance upon Arthas one day and find lasting freedom for her cursed people.

Varimathras - The dreadlord Varimathras was one of three demons appointed to rule over the Plaguelands on behalf of the Burning Legion. These dreadlords sought to overthrow the death knight Arthas and undo the power of the undead Scourge. Varimathras and his brethren coordinated their efforts with those of the banshee

Sylvanas Windrunner in an attempt to overthrow Arthas and claim Lordaeron. Though their plot worked as planned, Sylvanas turned on the dreadlords next. In order to save his own life, Varimathras was forced to swear allegiance to Sylvanas and her Forsaken warriors. Now he serves as her majordomo and works ceaselessly to safeguard the Undercity from all threats.

Master Apothecary Faranell - In life, Faranell was an alchemist of great renown and spent the better part of his days studying amongst the learned wizards of Dalaran. He enjoyed nothing more than experimenting with concoctions of every sort, always looking to create a serum for this, an antidote for that. After he died from the plague and rose as one of the Forsaken, his limitless curiosity was twisted by depthless sadism. Now Faranell uses his skills in service to Queen Sylvanas by crafting alchemical monstrosities and designing newer, more devastating plagues and toxins.

III. Glossary

These are common terms and acronyms used all the time in chat in World of Warcraft.

Common Terms

Add
An extra monster that joins an existing battle. This is often used as a warning by a group member: "Add!"

Alt
Other characters on your account besides the one you are currently playing. This is an abbreviation for alternate. Usually alt refers to any character other than your highest-level character.

Aggro
The act of a monster becoming hostile and attacking you. Often invoked when a player moves too close to a monster and unintentionally provokes it to attack. Aggro also refers to a monster's aggression level towards you.

Aggro Radius
The radius around a monster at which point you will provoke it to attack you. Aggro radius depends upon your level and the monster's level.

Agi
An abbreviation of agility.

Avatar
Your character.

Buff
A beneficial spell cast on a monster or player. An example of a buff is the mage's Arcane intellect.

Carebear
A disparaging term for a player that prefers to help other players attack monsters rather than attack other players in a player versus player environment. Usually this term is used by players who prefer PvP combat.

Caster
A character that primarily stays away from the front of combat in order to cast helpful spells on allies and harmful spells on enemies. Mages and priests are two examples of casters.

Combat Pet
An NPC controlled by a player that can fight monsters and assist the player and his party members.

Cooldown
The waiting time before an ability, skill, or spell can be used again.

Creep
A monster.

Critter
A creature that doesn't attack back, like a bunny or deer.

Debuff   A negative spell cast on a monster or player that weakens it. An example of a debuff is the warlock's curse of weakness.

Drop   The treasure left behind by a monster when you kill it. Used this way, it is synonymous with loot. Also a verb meaning the act of a monster leaving behind treasure.

Griefer   A person who purposely tries to annoy or anger other players.

Grinding   Staying in the same area fighting the same types of monsters for a very long time.

Hate   The amount of aggression, or aggro, a monster has built up against you. When a monster has more hate against you than any other surrounding players, it will attack you. Different actions, such as healing players or damaging the monster, will generate different levels of hate. Hate is synonymous with threat.

Incoming   It means an attack is coming. Sometimes abbreviated as inc.

Instance   A unique copy of a dungeon created when you and your group enter that dungeon. Only you and your group will be in your copy of the dungeon. Another group that enters the same area will enter their own copy of the dungeon.

Int   An abbreviation of intelligence.

Kiting   A style of combat in which a player continually stays out of combat range of an enemy, while simultaneously causing damage to it.

Log   Logging off or disconnecting from the game.

Loot   To take treasure from a monster corpse or object, such as a chest or box. Also used to mean the treasure itself.

Lvl   An abbreviation of level.

Mez   Any spell that temporarily incapacitates a target. Sometimes used as a verb to mean the act of incapacitating a target. An abbreviation of mesmerize.

Mob   Any computer-controlled character in the game, whether hostile or not. An abbreviation of mobile.

Newbie   Any new player to the game. Sometimes abbreviated as newb. Some players consider it a insulting term.

Pet   A non-combative NPC, such as a parrot, dog, or cat, controlled by a player.

Pop   Respawn.

Port   To transport yourself or other players to another location in the world through spells or abilities. An abbreviation of teleport.

Pull	To draw a monster away from its current location and back to the party. Pulling is done so that the party can fight individual monsters and not groups of them.
Puller	A player that pulls monsters for the party.
Raid	A large-scale attack on an area by a group of parties and players.
Res	An abbreviation of resurrect or resurrection.
Respawn	The act of a dead monster's spawning, or appearing, again. Also used to describe the respawned monster itself.
Spawn	The location or process of a monster or monsters appearing when they are created in the world.
Spi	An abbreviation of spirit.
Sta	An abbreviation of stamina.
Stack	A number of identical items placed in a single inventory slot to conserve space. Only certain items can be stacked.
Str	An abbreviation of strength.
Tank	A character that engages in melee with enemies and can withstand a lot of damage. Warriors and paladins are two examples of tanks. Also used as a verb to describe the act of engaging in melee with enemies.
Taunt	To provoke a monster into attacking your character, thereby pulling its attention away from its current target.
Threat	See Hate.
Train	To lead monsters so that they will attack another player.
Twink	A low-level character made more powerful by higher-level characters, usually through gifts of armor and weapons that the character would not normally have at such a low level. Also used as a verb to describe the act of giving low-level characters powerful items uncommon at their level.
XP	Experience points. Also called exp.

Acronyms

AC	Armor Class	MMORPG	Massively Multiplayer Online Role-Playing Game
AoE	Area of Effect	MT	Mistell
AE	Area Effect	NM	Never Mind
AFK	Away From Keyboard	NP	No Problem
BRB	Be Right Back	NPC	Non-Player Character
DD	Direct Damage	OOM	Out Of Mana
DOT	Damage Over Time	PC	Price Check
DPS	Damage Per Second	PC	Player Character
FH	Full Health	PK	Player Kill or Player Killer
FM	Full Mana	PST	Please Send Tell
FvF	Faction versus Faction	PvE	Player versus Environment
GM	Game Master	PvP	Player versus Player
GS	Goldshire	RH	Razor Hill
GTG	Good To Go	RR	Redridge
HP	Hit Points or Health Points	SW	Stormwind
IF	Ironforge	TB	Thunder Bluff
KS	Kill Stealing (or Kill Steal or Kill Stealer)	TY	Thank You
		UC	Undercity
LFG	Looking For Group	WF	Westfall
LFM	Looking For More	WB	Welcome Back
LOL	Laugh Out Loud	WoW	World of Warcraft
LOM	Low On Mana	WTB	Want To Buy
MMO	Massively-Multiplayer Online	WTS	Want To Sell
MMOG	Massively Multiplayer Online Game		

IV. Customer Support

If you encounter a problem with the game or with other players while playing World of Warcraft, you can contact a game master (GM) for support.

GMs are customer support representatives who are online 24 hours a day, seven days a week, to assist you with any trouble you experience in the game.

HOW TO CONTACT A GM

To contact a GM, click on the Help Request icon, which appears as a red question mark, at the bottom of your screen.

Clicking the Help Request button opens up the Help menu. There are three choices on the Help Request screen. You can make a suggestion, submit a bug, or page a GM. To contact a GM, choose the Page a GM option.

Contacting a GM in the Game

At the next screen, you will want to select the category that fits closest to the issue you are trying to report.

You will then be prompted to enter a subject for your ticket, and a description of your situation. Please try to be as descriptive as possible.

After typing your description and clicking the Submit button, a ticket appears at the upper right corner of your screen. This tells you that you have an active ticket and that a GM will contact you.

Once contacted, explain your situation to the GM. When the issue is resolved, the GM will erase the ticket from your screen.

Contacting a GM Outside the Game

If you cannot log into the game and wish to submit a concern to the GM staff, send an email to **WoWGM@blizzard.com** describing your problem in detail.

Identifying a GM

Game masters can be identified in-game by the GM tag that accompanies their player name. For example: <GM>Taredan

In addition, any message that a GM says in general or sends to you privately is prefaced with the "<GM>" tag. For example: "<GM> Junco whispers: Hello…"

GMs also look distinct, since they wear a unique game master uniform consisting of a dark blue robe that is unavailable to other players.

GM-related Issues

If you have a concern with a GM, or would like to send positive or negative feedback, please send an email to WoWGMConcerns@blizzard.com.

ACCOUNT ISSUES

If you have a problem with your account that prevents you from logging on, email **WoWAccountAdmin@blizzard.com** describing your problem. Some problems that the account administration handles are account disputes, hacking, and account closures by the GM department. For billing issues, you should email **Billing@blizzard.com**.

TECHNICAL SUPPORT

If you experience any technical difficulties while playing the game, please refer to the Troubleshooting and Technical Support section in Chapter 1: Installation.

The GM staff is not trained to handle technical support, so please contact the technical support staff if your problem cannot be resolved through the steps outlined in Chapter 1.

World of Warcraft Credits

Game Design
Blizzard Entertainment

Executive Producer
Mike Morhaime

Team Lead
Mark Kern

Art Director
William Petras

Creative Director
Chris Metzen

Lead Animator
Kevin Beardslee

Lead Artist
Justin Thavirat

Lead Character Artist
Brandon Idol

Lead Designers
Rob Pardo, Allen Adham

Lead Programmer
John Cash

Lead Technical Artist
Kyle Harrison

Producers
Shane Dabiri
Carlos Guerrero

Additional Production
Chris Sigaty

Programming
Jesse Blomberg
Dan Buckler
Robert Bridenbecker
Jeff Chow
Scott Hartin
Sam Lantinga
Twain Martin
Loren McQuade
Collin Murray
David Ray
Joe Rumsey
Derek Sakamoto
Tim Truesdale
Matthew Versluys
Jeremy Wood

Additional Programming
Andy Bond
Bob Fitch
Monte Krol
Graham Madarasz
Jay Patel

Install/Patch/Distribution Programming
Brian Fitzgerald
John Mikros
John Stiles
Tony Tribelli
Stephen C. Wong

Install/Patch/Distribution Producer
Derek Simmons

Macintosh Programming
John Mikros

Addiitonal Macintosh Programming
Rob Barris, John Stiles

Animators
Adam Byrne
Jay Hathaway
Eric Henze
Solomon Lee

Dungeon/City Artists
Jose Aello, Jr.
Roger Eberhart
Dana Jan
Aaron Keller
Jimmy Lo
Matt Mocarski
Brian Morrisroe
Jamin Shoulet
John Staats

World Content Artists
Carlo Arellano
Sam Didier
Brian Hsu
Roman Kenney
Maxx Marshall
Matt Milizia
Dan Moore
Ted Park
Gary Platner

Technical Artist
Peter Underwood

Exterior Level Designers
Bo Bell
James Chadwick
Mark Downie
Alen Lapidis
Matt Sanders

Additional Art
Dave Berggren
Allen Dilling
Toph Gorham
Trevor Jacobs
Tom Jung
Cameron Lamprecht
Rob McNaughton
Mickey Nielson
Matt Oursbourn

Game Designers
Tom Chilton
Eric Dodds
Michael Heiberg
Kevin Jordan
Jeffrey Kaplan
John Yoo

Quest Designers
Alex Afrasiabi
Michael Backus
Suzanne Brownell
Shawn Carnes
Michael Chu
Jeffrey Kaplan
Pat Nagle

World Designers
Geoff Goodman
Andy Kirton
Joshua Kurtz
Steven Pierce

Additional Design
Tom Cadwell
Dave Fried
Dave Hale
Eric Maloof
Scott Mercer
Matt Morris
Jennifer Powell
Dean Shipley

Roseman, Chuck Salzman, David Sanchez, Samuel Schrimsher, Michael Schwan, Anant Singh, Brian Stankowitz, Shawn Su, Michael Mooteh Sun, Alex Tsang, Joseph Vales, Brandan Vanderpool, Sean Wang, Geoffrey Yeh, Tengying Yu

Additional Game Testing
Zach Allen, Zebulon Batke, Josh Bertram, Zach Callanan, Wesley Campbell, Greg Cucchissi, Dustin Chang, Yuan Cheng, Jack Cheung, Joel Clift, Matt Coalson, Beni Elgueta, Dave Eliasberg, Brian Fattorini, Gary Gibson, Manuel Gonzales, Justin Hamilton, Jason Thor Hall, Patrick Henry, Lyno Hychong, Jeff Jones, Stephen Kim, Jason Liang, Richard Lin, Robert Lohaus, John Meyers, Brandon Norton, Haz Novoa, Wale Oyejide, David Potts, Emilio Segura, Kenneth Shaw, Steve Shin, Geordie Swainbank, Walter Takata, Joshua Tapley, Jeffrey Therrien, Ian Welke, Christopher Van Der Westhuizen, Constance Wang, Daniel Westmoreland

Technical Support Manager
Thor Biafore

Assistant Technical Support Manager
Jason Stilwell

Billing and Account Services Lead
Doug Abel

Sales/Billing
Liam Knapp, Dean Sheldon, Jason White

Technical Support Programming
David Nguyen

Technical Support Representatives
Charlie Areson, Jason Chen, Brett Dixon, Norman Harms, Joseph Holley, John Hsieh, Chad Jones, Jeff Jones, Richard Kennedy, Nathan Lutsock, Chris Nedrebo, Michael Nguyen, Michael Pierce, Cuong Quach, Adam Slack, Scott Sweeting, Martin Tande, Micah Whipple, Mataio Wilson, Jamie Wood, Kenny Zigler

In-Game Support Management
Eric Avila

In-Game Support Leads
Mitchell Bricker, Chris Manley, Jason Park, John Schwartz, Max Whitaker

In-Game Support
Dustin Chang, Jeremy Conrad, Josh Downs, Nathan Erickson, Bejan Fozdar, Justin Goad, Manuel Gonzales, Ryan Gunst, Justin Guthrie, Kristen Hewes, Danielle Homer, Tony Hsu, Bryan Langford, Corey Louie, Mark McCarty, Travis Otten, Kyle Riseling, Trevor Rothman, Julie Sklarew, Brian Smith, Laura Szigeti, Asheesh Thukral, Chris Voss, Oliver Voss, David Wareham

Localization Producer
Jason Hutchins

Associate Localization Producer
Jonas Laster

VUG LOCALIZATION TEAM

General Manager
Gerry Carty

European Localisation Manager
Barry Kehoe

Senior Project Manag
Eithne Hagan

Translation Vendor Manager
Annette Lee

Linguistic Project Manager
Laura Casanellas

Linguistic Coordinate
Corina Zaha

Engineering Manager
Lawrence Moran

Senior Engineer
David Doheny

Q.A. Manager
David Hickey

Senior Q.A. Lead
Conor Harlow

Q.A. Testers - French
Maurice Larkin
Russell Perin
Dimitry Renardet

Q.A. Testers - German
Sandra Rothig
Henry Ertner
Hugh Lawton

Graphics/Audio Coordination
Bill Sweeney
David Fleming

RTM Validation
Philippe Gendreau

BLIZZARD ENTERTAINMENT

Business Developme & Business Operation
Paul Sams

Business Developme & Operations
Elaine Dilorio, Denise Lop Isaac Matarasso, Lisa Pear Sarah Tucker

Information Technologies Manag
Robert Van Dusen

Information Technologies
Edward Hanes, Brian Hill, Mike Kramer, Hung Nguyen, Mike Pearce, Mike Schaefer, Jeremy Smith, Casey Suyeto, Stephen T. Wong

IT Engineering & Network Design
Adrian Luff, Jeff Berube

Data Archivist
Cris Mackey

Office Administration/ Human Resources/ Facilities Management
Stacy Dishon, Jeanette Bullock, Kaeo Milker, Jamie Deveaux, Hugh Todd, Talishia Thompson

Financial Management
David Gee, Paul Sams

Public Relations
Lisa Bucek-Jensen, Ellliott Chin, Gil Shif, George Wang

Web Team
Lisa Bucek-Jensen, Mathieu Chauvin, Geoff Fraizer, Mike Rein, Jon Jelinek, Gil Shif, Alex Sun, Blaine Whittle

Community Management
Lisa Bucek-Jensen, Daniel Chin, Paul Della Bitta, Gil Shif

Legal Counsel
Kevin Crook, Terri Durham, Rod Rigole, Eric Roeder, Tracy Gibbs-Sargeant, James Shaw

Global Brand Management
Neal Hubbard, Marc Hutcheson, Matt Kassan

North American Sales
Philip O'Neil, Bruce Slywka, Lowell Vaughen

Marketing Creative Services
Cathy Carter-Humphreys, Jessica Drossin, Zachary Hubert, Steve Parker, Raul Ramirez, Hayley Sumner, Bill Watt

Recruiting
Jack Sterling

Packaging Artwork
William Petras, Justin Thavirat

Manufacturing
Tom Bryan, Bob Wharton

Hosting Partners
AT&T, DACOM/KIDC, Telia

Director of Dunsel Development
Frank Pearce

Dunsel Specialist
Alan Dabiri

Thanks To
Chris Sigaty
Kirk Mahony
Jimmie Nelson
Donna Anthony
Beau Yarborough
Ian Welke
Christophe Ramboz
Michael Fuller
Flavie Gufflet
Stu Rose
Duane Stinnett
Brenda Perdion

Special Thanks
Blizzard North
Bruce Hack
Jean-Francois Grollemund
Bob & Jan Davidson

Cinematic Sound Contractors
David Farmer, Paul Menichini, Jeff Kurtenacker, Michael Aarvold, Robert Michael Sherlock, Tom Brewer

Original choir music performed by the University Choir & California State University, Long Beach Original music recorded at Citrus College, Glendora, CA

WE WANT TO EXTEND A VERY SPECIAL THANKS TO ALL OUR FAMILIES. YOUR NEVER-ENDING PATIENCE AND UNDERSTANDING MADE IT ALL POSSIBLE. WE LOVE YOU!

Additional Thanks
Celeste Aviva, Tracy Farr, Amber Ray, Tiffany and Taylor Hayes, Andrea Lobo, The Idols & Pat Morrison, Shane Hensley, Michele Henze, Claudia & Alanna Guerrero, My brother Brad…we all need heroes, Kim & Ashley Bridenbecker, Alexander K. Lee, The Chosen & Bill, Peter Milizia, The Petras Family, Rob Chacko, Kandice Murray, Michelle Delgado, The Thavirats & Corinna Lee, Kayla Hong-Tim Nguyen, Mike Phillips, Cathy Tsai and The Chow Family, Suzanne Di Piazza, Pooka, Kerri Jaquith Simmons, Patricia, Nate, Chris, Matt & Jenna, Laura Szigeti, Sofia Vergara, Sarah Arellano, Olivia Lee Heiberg, Nikita Mikros, April & Sofia Metzen, Girls of Starbucks, Mary, Johnny, and Joey Cash, Katherine & Penelope Jordan, Danna, Jessica, Tisa, Jade and Breanna, Gammaray Helen Mckenney, Bill & Kathie Blomberg, The Sakamoto Family, Nick "Blood Angel" Betteker, Angelista, Napoleon Dynamite, Joohyun Lee, April and Noah Beardslee, Dawn Marshall, Mandilynn Weygandt, Stephanie Keefer, the good people of The Daily Blab, Ed, May, & Sheryl Narahara, Arleen Powell, Andrew Thorson, Imelda & Alex Kern, Olivia Lee, Peter Jackson, Victoria, Garrett, & Cassandra, Katherine Jordan, Gina MacGregor, Karen & Julia Barris, The Infamous

Kitt3n, Hilary & F.C. Carnes, Happy 30th to RUSH, Lara Lee, Brenda Perdion, Tina & Melissa Maloof, The Pearce Family, Smoove TB, The Bandit, The PUNisher, The Leaky Faucet, T. Blave, The Censor, Susan, Matthew & Michael Sams, Megan Wooley, Tina Chan, Stacey Frayne, Haibo Li, Katelynn Hassler, Lucianna Kochnoff, Shelly Mead, Debbie Lanz, Jessica Ellis, Khana Le, Brian Flora, Chen Bin Hua, The Price Family, Deana Matarasso, Harminder Brar, The McCoy Family, The Yu Family, The Wang Family, The Samia Family, The Chamberlain Family, The Burnett Family, The Haskell Family, The Dai Family, The Peterson Family, The Carpenter Family, Joe "Vargen" Biafore, Beverly & Shangreaux Lagrave, Dee Ann Fifer, Riley & The Sigaty Family, Melissa Huggins, Laura Clifton, Jason & Damian Hall, Koren Buckner, Gali Mehl, The Ben-Bassat Family, David, Cameron & Brianna Di Iorio, Nicole Hamelin, Matt, Shaun & Amanda Smiley, Ty, Noel & Marge Williams, Silvia, Kai, and Kiana Van Dusen, Astrid and K.C. Ross, Janée Laster, Everyone at Hewlett-Packard, Everyone at Cisco.

BLIZZARD
EUROPE TEAM

Sales, Marketing & PR
Cédric Maréchal
Anne Bérard
Julia Gastaldi
Eric Chauveau
Yann Pallatier
Guillaume Sartre
Martin Leidenfrost
Prune Moldawan
Sebastien Garnault

Business Development/Finance
Delphine Le Corre
Benoit Mechineau
Benoit Dufor

Technical Team
Jean-Michel Courivaud
Julien Mariani
Steve Viegas
Philippe Peeters
Mathieu Chauvin

Support Services
Frederic Menou
Christian Scharling
Emmanuel Obert

BLIZZARD
KOREA TEAM

Sales, Marketing & PR
Richard Kwon
Patrick Lee
Christy Um
Hyejin Yum
Jinkyu Ko
Yungjoo Ko
Sam Ohn
Steve Kang

Business Development
Tommy Park
Mac Kwon

Operations
Jungwon Hahn
Taewon Yun
Changuk Park

Network Operations
Sungsoo Khim
Sangyong Park
Minhong Kim
Manjung Ha

Technical Team
Jiwoong Kim
Joonho Lee
Juno Kwak
Hyunjoo Song
Jonghyuk Lee
Hanbaek Choi
Sangeun Gu
Jean Park
Seungki Choi
Hyojin Bae
Dohyeong Kim
Eunjin Kim

Support Services
James Kim
Jeongwon Min
Kumshim Shin
Bum Choi
Young Namgoong
Wonjong Lee
Hyunshin Lim
Jihun Lee
Jiyoon Kim
Eunjung Lee
Jinman Park
Yooseok Pan
Taehee Kang
Jinsun Park
Yongjo Choi
Hosung Lee
Eunyoung Park
Jaehong Jeong
Minsun Back
Yoonhee Kim
Dongkyun Kang
Kyunghyo Kim
Hyojin Kim
Kyungtae Myung
sungho Eom
Jaebum Ahn
Aungoun Lee
Jungjun Lee
Sanhak Jeon
Chulsoo Jung

Finance & Administration
Ahlim Kim
Kate Kim
Okyoung Lee
Chami Kang
Junghoon Kim
Hyunjung Noh

Asia Pacific HQ
Hubert Larenaudie
Franck Villet
Mark Warburton
Chris Ansell
Kim Watt
Michael Tan
Steve Voorma

YOU SHOULD CAREFULLY READ THE FOLLOWING END USER LICENSE AGREEMENT BEFORE INSTALLING THIS SOFTWARE PROGRAM. BY INSTALLING, COPYING, OR OTHERWISE USING THE SOFTWARE PROGRAM, YOU AGREE TO BE BOUND BY THE TERMS OF THIS AGREEMENT. IF YOU DO NOT AGREE TO THE TERMS OF THIS AGREEMENT, PROMPTLY RETURN THE UNUSED SOFTWARE PROGRAM TO THE PLACE OF PURCHASE, OR CONTACT BLIZZARD CUSTOMER SERVICE AT (800) 592-5499 FOR A FULL REFUND OF THE PURCHASE PRICE WITHIN 30 DAYS OF THE ORIGINAL PURCHASE.

END USER LICENSE AGREEMENT

This software program on CD-ROM, and any files that are delivered to you by Blizzard (via on-line transmission or otherwise) to "patch," update, or otherwise modify the software program, as well as any printed materials and any on-line or electronic documentation (the "Manual"), and any and all copies and derivative works of such software program and materials (collectively, with the "Game Client" defined below, the "Game") are the copyrighted work of Blizzard Entertainment, a division of Davidson & Associates, Inc. or its suppliers and licensors (collectively referred to herein as "Licensor"). All use of the Game is governed by the terms of this End User License Agreement ("License Agreement" or "Agreement"). The Game may only be played by obtaining from Licensor access to the World of Warcraft massively multi-player on-line role-playing game service (the "Service"), which is subject to a separate Terms of Use agreement (the "Terms of Use"). If your purchase of the Game included a period of "free access" to the Service, the Terms of Use agreement also governs your access to the Service during the period of "free access." The Game is distributed solely for use by authorized end users according to the terms of the License Agreement. Any use, reproduction or redistribution of the Game not expressly authorized by the terms of the License Agreement is expressly prohibited.

1. Grant of a Limited Use License. The Game installs computer software (hereafter referred to as the "Game Client") onto your hardware to allow you to play the Game through your account with the Service (your "Account"). Licensor hereby grants, and by installing the Game Client you thereby accept, a limited, non-exclusive license and right to install the Game Client for your personal use on one (1) or more computers which you own or which are under your personal control. All use of the Game Client is subject to this License Agreement and to the Terms of Use agreement, which you must accept before you can use your Account to play the Game through access to the Service. Licensor reserves the right to update, modify or change the Terms of Use at any time.

2. Service and Terms of Use. As mentioned above, you must accept the Terms of Use in order to access the Service to play the Game. The Terms of Use agreement governs all aspects of game play. You may view the Terms of Use by visiting the following website: http://www.worldofwarcraft.com/legal/termsofuse.shtml. If you do not agree with the Terms of Use, then (i) you should not register for an Account to play the Game, and (ii) you should contact Licensor's customer service at (800) 592-5499 to arrange to return the Game for a full refund of the purchase price within thirty (30) days of the original purchase. Once you accept the Terms of Use and register an Account, the purchase price of the Game will not be refunded to you if you choose not to continue the monthly subscription to the Service.

3. Ownership.

  A. All title, ownership rights and intellectual property rights in and to the Game and all copies thereof (including, but not limited to, any titles, computer code, themes, objects, characters, character names, stories, dialog, catch phrases, locations, concepts, artwork, character inventories, structural or landscape designs, animations, sounds, musical compositions, audio-visual effects, storylines, character likenesses, methods of operation, moral rights, any related documentation, and "applets" incorporated into the Game) are owned or expressly licensed by Licensor. The Game is protected by the copyright laws of the United States, international copyright treaties and conventions, and other laws. All rights are reserved. The Game may contain certain licensed materials, and the licensors of those materials may enforce their rights in the event of any violation of this License Agreement.

   B. You may permanently transfer ownership of the Game and all parts thereof, and all of your rights and obligations under the License Agreement, to another by physically transferring the CD-ROM, all original packaging, and all Manuals or other documentation associated with the Game, and by removing from all of your home or personal computers and destroying any remaining materials concerning the Game in your possession or control, provided the recipient agrees to the terms of this License Agreement. The transferor (i.e., you), and not the Licensor, agrees to be solely responsible for any taxes, fees, charges, duties, withholdings, assessments, and the like, together with any interest, penalties, and additions imposed in connection with such transfer.

4. Responsibilities of End User.

   A. Subject to the Grant of License hereinabove, you may not, in whole or in part, copy, photocopy, reproduce, translate, reverse engineer, derive source code, modify, disassemble, decompile, or create derivative works based on the Game, or remove any proprietary notices or labels on the Game. Failure to comply with the restrictions and limitations contained in this Section 4 shall result in immediate, automatic termination of the license granted hereunder and may subject you to civil and/or criminal liability. Notwithstanding the foregoing, you may make one (1) copy of the Game Client and the Manuals for archival purposes only.

   B. You agree that you shall not, under any circumstances,

(i) sell, grant a security interest in or transfer reproductions of the Game to other parties in any way not expressly authorized herein, nor shall you rent, lease or license the Game to others;

(ii) exploit the Game or any of its parts, including, but not limited to, the Game Client, for any commercial purpose, including, but not limited to, use at a cyber café, computer gaming center or any other location-based site without the express written consent of Blizzard;

(iii) host, provide or develop matchmaking services for the Game or intercept, emulate or redirect the communication protocols used by Licensor in any way, including, without limitation, through protocol emulation, tunneling, packet sniffing, modifying or adding components to the Game, use of a utility program or any other techniques now known or hereafter developed, for any purpose, including, but not limited to, unauthorized network play over the Internet, network play utilizing commercial or non-commercial gaming networks or as part of content aggregation networks; or

(iv) create or maintain, under any circumstance, any unauthorized connections to the Game or the Service. All connections to the Game and/or the Service, whether created by the Game Client or by other tools and utilities, may only be made through methods and means expressly approved by Licensor. Under no circumstances may you connect, or create tools that allow you or others to connect, to the Game's proprietary interface or interfaces other than those expressly provided by Licensor for public use.

5. Termination. This License Agreement is effective until terminated. You may terminate the License Agreement at any time by (i) destroying the Game; (ii) removing the Game Client from your hard drive; and (iii) notifying Licensor of your intention to terminate this License Agreement. Licensor may, at its discretion, terminate this License Agreement in the event that you fail to comply with the terms and conditions contained herein, or the terms and conditions contained in the Terms of Use. In such event, you must immediately destroy the Game and remove the Game Client from your hard drive. Upon termination of this Agreement for any reason, all licenses granted herein shall immediately terminate.

6. Export Controls. The Game may not be re-exported, downloaded or otherwise exported into (or to a national or resident of) any country to which the U.S. has embargoed goods, or to anyone on the U.S. Treasury Department's list of Specially Designated Nationals or the U.S. Commerce Department's Table of Denial Orders. By installing the Game, you are agreeing to the foregoing, and you are representing and warranting that you are not located in, under the control of, or a national or resident of any such country or on any such list.

7. Patches and Updates. Licensor may deploy or provide patches, updates and modifications to the Game that must be installed for the user to continue to play the Game. Licensor may update the Game remotely, including, without limitation, the Game Client residing on the user's machine, without knowledge or consent of the user, and you hereby grant to Licensor your consent to deploy and apply such patches, updates and modifications to the Game.

8. Duration of the "On-line" Component of the Game. This Game is an 'on-line' game that must be played over the Internet through the Service, as provided by Licensor. You understand and agree that the Service is provided by Licensor at its discretion and may be terminated or otherwise discontinued by Licensor pursuant to the Terms of Use.

9. Limited Warranty. Licensor expressly disclaims any warranty for the Game, including the Game Client and Manual(s). THE GAME, GAME CLIENT AND MANUAL(S) ARE PROVIDED "AS IS" WITHOUT WARRANTY OF ANY KIND, EITHER EXPRESS OR IMPLIED, INCLUDING, WITHOUT LIMITATION, ANY IMPLIED WARRANTIES OF CONDITION, DEFECTS, USE, MERCHANTABILITY, FITNESS FOR A PARTICULAR PURPOSE OR USE, OR NONINFRINGEMENT. The entire risk arising out of use or performance of the Game, Game Client and Manual(s) remains with the user. Notwithstanding the foregoing, Licensor warrants up to and including 90 days from the date of your purchase of the Game that the media containing the Game Client shall be free from defects in material and workmanship. In the event that such media proves to be defective during that time period, and upon presentation to Licensor of proof of purchase of the defective media, Licensor will at its option 1) correct any defect, 2) provide you with a product of equal or lesser value, or 3) refund your money. THE FOREGOING IS YOUR SOLE AND EXCLUSIVE REMEDY FOR THE EXPRESS WARRANTY SET FORTH IN THIS SECTION. SOME STATES DO NOT ALLOW THE EXCLUSION OR LIMITATION OF IMPLIED WARRANTIES OR LIABILITY FOR INCIDENTAL DAMAGES, SO THE ABOVE LIMITATIONS MAY NOT APPLY TO YOU.

10. Limitation of Liability. NEITHER LICENSOR NOR ITS PARENT, SUBSIDIARIES OR AFFILIATES SHALL BE LIABLE IN ANY WAY FOR LOSS OR DAMAGE OF ANY KIND RESULTING FROM THE USE OF THE GAME, INCLUDING, BUT NOT LIMITED TO, LOSS OF DATA, LOSS OF GOODWILL, WORK STOPPAGE, COMPUTER FAILURE OR MALFUNCTION, OR ANY AND ALL OTHER DAMAGES OR LOSSES. ANY WARRANTY AGAINST INFRINGE-MENT THAT MAY BE PROVIDED IN SECTION 2-312(3) OF THE UNIFORM COMMERCIAL CODE AND/OR IN ANY OTHER COMPARABLE STATE STATUTE IS EXPRESSLY DISCLAIMED. FURTHER, LICENSOR SHALL NOT BE LIABLE IN ANY WAY FOR THE LOSS OR DAMAGE TO PLAYER CHARACTERS, ACCOUNTS, STATISTICS OR USER PROFILE INFORMATION STORED BY THE GAME AND/OR THE SERVICE. LICENSOR SHALL NOT BE RESPONSIBLE FOR ANY INTERRUPTIONS OF SERVICE, INCLUDING, BUT NOT LIMITED TO, ISP DISRUPTIONS, SOFTWARE OR HARDWARE FAILURES OR ANY OTHER EVENT WHICH MAY RESULT IN A LOSS OF DATA OR DISRUPTION OF SERVICE. IN NO EVENT WILL LICENSOR BE LIABLE TO YOU FOR ANY INDIRECT, INCIDENTAL, SPECIAL, EXEMPLARY OR CONSEQUENTIAL DAMAGES. Some states do not allow the exclusion or limitation of incidental or consequential damages, or allow limitations on how long an implied warranty lasts, so the above limitations may not apply to you.

11. Equitable Remedies. You hereby agree that Licensor would be irreparably damaged if the terms of this License Agreement were not specifically enforced, and therefore you agree that Licensor shall be entitled, without bond, other security, or proof of damages, to appropriate equitable remedies with respect to breaches of this License Agreement, in addition to such other remedies as Licensor may otherwise have available to it under applicable laws. In the event any litigation is brought by either party in connection with this License Agreement, the prevailing party in such litigation shall be entitled to recover from the other party all the costs, attorneys' fees and other expenses incurred by such prevailing party in the litigation.

12. Changes to the Agreement. Blizzard reserves the right, at its sole discretion, to change, modify, add to, supplement or delete any of the terms and conditions of this License Agreement when Blizzard upgrades the Game Client, effective upon prior notice as follows: Blizzard will post notification of any such changes to this License Agreement on the World of Warcraft website and will post the revised version of this License Agreement in this location, and may provide such other notice as Blizzard may elect in its sole discretion, which may include by email, postal mail or pop-up screen. If any future changes to this License Agreement are unacceptable to you or cause you to no longer be in compliance with this License Agreement, you may terminate this License Agreement in accordance with Section 5 herein. Your installation and use of any updated or modifications to the Game or your continued use of the Game following notice of changes to this Agreement as described above will mean you accept any and all such changes. Blizzard may change, modify, suspend, or discontinue any aspect of the Game at any time. Blizzard may also impose limits on certain features or restrict your access to parts or all of the Game without notice or liability. You have no interest, monetary or otherwise, in any feature or content contained in the Game.

13. Miscellaneous. This License Agreement shall be deemed to have been made and executed in the State of California without regard to conflicts of law provisions, and any dispute arising hereunder shall be resolved in accordance with the law of California. You agree that any claim asserted in any legal proceeding by one of the parties against the other shall be commenced and maintained in any state or federal court located in the State of California, County of Los Angeles, having subject matter jurisdiction with respect to the dispute between the parties. In the event that any provision of this License Agreement shall be held by a court or other tribunal of competent jurisdiction to be unenforceable, such provision will be enforced to the maximum extent permissible, and the remaining portions of this License Agreement shall remain in full force and effect. This License Agreement constitutes and contains the entire agreement between the parties with respect to the subject matter hereof and supersedes any prior oral or written agreements, provided, however, that this Agreement shall coexist with, and shall not supersede, the Terms of Use. To the extent that the provisions of this Agreement conflict with the provisions of the Terms of Use, the conflicting provisions in the Terms of Use shall govern. I hereby acknowledge that I have read and understand the foregoing License Agreement and agree that the action of installing the Game Client is an acknowledgment of my agreement to be bound by the terms and conditions of the License Agreement contained herein.